International Television Co-Production

George –

With much appreciation for all your work in the communications field

Carla
8/7/92

RELATED FOCAL PRESS TITLES

International Television Co-Production

From Access to Success

Carla B. Johnston

Focal Press
Boston London

Focal Press is an imprint of Butterworth-Heinemann.

Copyright © 1992 by Butterworth-Heinemann, a division of Reed Publishing (USA) Inc. All rights reserved.

Recognizing the importance of preserving what has been written, it is the policy of Butterworth-Heinemann to have the books it publishes printed on acid-free paper, and we exert our best efforts to that end.

Library of Congress Cataloging-in-Publication Data
Johnston, Carla B.
    International television co-production : from access to success /
Carla B. Johnston.
        p. cm.
    Includes bibliographical references and index.
    ISBN 0-240-80110-5 (pbk. : acid-free paper)
    1. Television—Production and direction.   2. Television
broadcasting—Economic aspects.   I. Title.
PN1995.9P7J64   1992
791.45'0232—dc20   92-16767
                                                        CIP

British Library Cataloguing in Publication Data
A catalogue record for this book is available from the British Library.

Butterworth-Heinemann
80 Montvale Avenue
Stoneham, MA 02180

10 9 8 7 6 5 4 3 2 1

Printed in the United States of America

To the entrepreneur in international television co-production. May you make not just a name, money, and a career. May you make a difference.

Contents

Acknowledgments

This book is for the professional wanting information, resources, and contacts helpful to setting a direction for one's career. It is for the person interested in the big picture—the many ways to engage in international television co-production.

My purpose in writing this book is to identify the unprecedented opportunity available in international television co-production. As the page of history turns to a new century, we find ourselves living ever closer to the "global village." Technological tools are excellent. Policy and management tools such as co-production offer new flexibility. The examples, suggestions, and contacts in this book are intended as a practical guide for the innovator in television production.

The book could not have been written without the help of many individuals. A hearty thank you to Lydia Stephans, Director of Programming, ABC Sports, New York; Dr. Leonid A. Zolotarevsky, Director, International Relations Department, U.S.S.R. National State Broadcasting Company, Moscow; Herb Fuller, independent filmmaker, Boston; Meg Gottemoeller, President, World Information Corporation, New York; Richard Sydenham, Producer, Special Programs Section, Department of Information, United Nations, New York; Pierre Brunel-Lantenac, Director, News Operations, European Broadcasting Union, Geneva; Tieneke de Nooj, Producer, Radio Television Luxembourg, Hilversum, The Netherlands; Dighton E. Spooner, Jr., Executive Vice President, Films for Television, Grenada Television, London; Dr. Annette Wachter, Director of Strategic Planning, West Deutscher Rundfunk, Koln, Germany; Dr. Manfred Jenke, Director of Broadcasting, West Deutscher Rundfunk, Koln, Germany; Alain Jehlan, Director of Acquisitions, "Nova," WGBH, Boston; Jim Stevenson, Chief Executive, Educational Broadcasting Services Trust, London; Eric Johnston, President, Johnston and Associates, Boston; Dr. Milan Smid, Assistant Professor, Electronic Media Department, Charles University, Prague, Czechoslovakia; Elsabe Wessels, M-NET TV Political Correspondent, Johannesburg, South Africa; Mitch Abel, Director of Video Transfer Services, New England Telephone, Boston; Susan Ryan, Independent Distribution Consultant, New York; Bob Michelson, Photos by Michelson, Braintree, Massachusetts; and Claire Andrade Watkins, Wellesley, College, Wellesley, Massachusetts, for their contributions to the content of the book.

My special thanks to John and Shiela Barbetta, Emerson College's Kasteel Well, The Netherlands, for providing the delightful physical and social environment in which I could work on the manuscript. Without the confidence and ongoing assistance of editors Karen Speerstra, Phil Sutherland, and Evelyn Laiacona, I'm certain

there would never have been a finished product. Thanks to John Davis, Debbi, and Elise, whose facts, fun, critiques, and general confidence can be found behind the pages and between the lines. And to Bob Hilliard, much appreciation for the unceasing encouragement and hours of time reading manuscripts.

1

▼ Why Co-Production?

*Television is a way of communicating—either through entertainment,
or through sports as a passion, or to show what's going on in the rest
of the world. The only way you can show what's going on in the rest of
the world is by collaborating internationally.*[1]
— *Lydia Stephans, Director of Programming, ABC Sports*

During the last two decades of the 20th century we have all moved from our old familiar neighborhoods to a new neighborhood—a global neighborhood. The new communication technologies combined with the political and economic shifts during these two decades are responsible for this change in the world's lifestyle.

Television is the vehicle that transported us from the old to the new and the vehicle through which we are meeting our new neighbors. Increasingly, television programs are seen across borders, programs are distributed internationally, and more and more programs are co-produced.

The video producer who wants to survive in this new and emerging society must (1) understand what's happening in the rapidly developing business of international television co-production, (2) identify specific career opportunities, and (3) see the potential that international co-production offers to those who will be the architects of the 21st century.

WHAT IS INTERNATIONAL CO-PRODUCTION?

Co-production is a tool for those individuals interested in providing a balanced flow of information to people across national borders within manageable budget limits. Once one has a focus for a career in international television and an idea for a program that might help one accomplish one's career objectives, co-production can be a tool for maximizing the results.

For our purposes, it entails (a) collaborative efforts to make television accessible across international borders, (b) cooperative efforts where nationals of more than one country are involved in one or more of the tasks—financing, script writing, pre-production, production, post-production, and distribution of television programming.

Co-production experiments have taken place for several decades, motivated both by the desire to cut production costs and by the desire to produce programs on topics otherwise not available. Now, as we embark on the 21st century, the full potential of this tool is becoming clearer.

WHY EXAMINE OPPORTUNITIES IN INTERNATIONAL CO-PRODUCTION?

Dr. Leonid A. Zolotarevsky, Director of the Department for International Programming, Russian National State Broadcasting Company (Gosteleradio), and Director of Sovtelexport, the new self-financed distribution and international co-production arm of Gosteleradio, provides a succinct answer to the question of why co-produce: "Television is the most efficient media for establishing direct contacts between people of different countries. It's not purely business; it's something more. It's not purely political; it's of a humanitarian nature. A devotion to humanitarian aids and ideals is the most important thing to begin with."[2]

While one must be careful to avoid the problems of cultural imperialism—saturation of programming from one culture (often American culture) that undercuts the unique heritage of other cultures, legitimate co-production can serve an important role for the advancement of global understanding and the liberation of people from oppression, and it can be an economic cornerstone for both micro and macro levels of the communications industry.

Since the people of Ireland have been able to watch the World Cup soccer match via satellite television transmission, the Archbishop of Dublin will never again be successful if he tries to dictate to the people that it is wrong to watch a country with a different political ideology play football. In 1950, Archbishop McQuaid actually restrained fans from attending a match against Godless Yugoslavia. Today the World Cup plays an important role in enabling global neighbors to get acquainted.

In former East Germany, prohibited otherwise from access to the Western world from 1945 until 1989, West German television showed a different version of the news from that shown on East German television. The people watched both, made their own evaluations, and acted accordingly. In 1989, East German television showed the parades and political speeches lauding the fortieth anniversary of the incumbent repressive political regime. West German television showed the first waves of dissatisfied East Germans refusing to go home from Hungary—protected by the Hungarian government. It was the first time in a generation that citizens had any way out of the Eastern block countries without risking their lives. West German TV also showed dissidents protesting the fortieth anniversary events. From this window to the West, countless East Germans saw the tide changing and mustered their own courage to join the call for change—simultaneously in communities across the country. Repressive government was overthrown.[3]

Global economic interdependence is a reality as we enter the 21st century. Multinational corporations know no boundaries. Economic growth, economic recession or depression, and environmental disrespect in one part of the world invariably affect the lifestyle of people living in other countries—in terms of standard of living, access to consumer goods, possibilities for a healthy environment, and refugee movements.

International television, especially when co-produced, can provide a form of economic development. Observe the efforts of the European Community to compete

with Hollywood and the efforts of the Japanese to develop joint ownership ventures with Hollywood. In the early 1990s international television syndication and co-ventures became important even to big budget entertainment entities like the Kirch Group, Viacom Broadcast and Entertainment, Capital Cities/ABC, CNN International, USA Network's Science Fiction Channel, Turner Broadcasting's 1992 launched cartoon network and the new E! Entertainment Television pay movie channel in Scandinavia and Benelux.[4] International television can provide an educational and corporate tool for enhancing the skill level of workers pursuing economic success in their own country. Television documentaries can provide the base of information needed to understand specific economic, environmental, and political problems so that support for solving these problems can develop.

In the words of one independent producer, "the flow of information has helped to stabilize the world. What more important reason could there be for promoting co-production?"[5]

HOW THIS BOOK IS ORGANIZED

Chapter 2 focuses on examples of innovative international television and types of co-productions. Chapter 3 addresses the legal, political, and economic realities of co-production. Chapter 4 focuses on the production process as well as cultural and technological influences on production. In Chapter 5, the reader will learn about the process of acquisition and distribution of internationally co-produced programs. Chapter 6 provides information and contacts for the person wishing to use the tool of co-production to accomplish her or his professional objectives. Chapter 7 summarizes by looking at trends and making some observations.

Notes

1. Personal interview with Lydia Stephans, Director, Programming, ABC Sports, 47 West 66th Street, New York, NY 10023, tel.: 212-456-3702, August 23, 1991.
2. Personal interview with Dr. Leonid A. Zolotarevsky, Director, Department for International Programming, U.S.S.R. National State Broadcasting Company, Moscow, Russia, June 13, 1991.
3. Dieter, Buhl, "Window to the West: How Television from the Federal Republic Influenced Events in East Germany," an occasional paper of The Shorenstein Barone Center for Press, Politics and Public Policy, Kennedy School of Government, Harvard University, late 1990(?) no date on publication.
4. Amdur, Meredith, "Shrinking Budgets Make for Smaller World," *Broadcasting,* Vol. 122, No. 17, April 20, 1992, p. 37f.
5. Personal interview with Herb Fuller, independent filmmaker, 54 Preston Road, Somerville, MA 02143, August 13, 1991.

2

Innovative Television
Co-Production Samples

In order to fully appreciate the opportunities that the tool of co-production can provide, let's look at some examples of creative communication through international television. Three unique models for 21st century communication: space bridges, teleconferencing, and collaborative news productions. In addition, co-productions may be made in the more traditional television programming formats of news, sports, entertainment, documentaries, educational, and corporate television.

THREE EXPERIMENTS

Space Bridges

The 1982 satellite linking of a San Bernardino, California, rock concert with a concert of rock musicians playing in the studios of the Soviet State Committee for Radio and Television Broadcasting in Moscow inaugurated a new form of person-to-person communication.[1] Over the following decade more than 20 *Space Bridges* occurred, including "Nova Space Bridge"—a joint discussion of Soviet and American scientists—two "Citizens' Summits," with open studio audiences in both the United States and the Soviet Union, and "Capital to Capital"—a program focusing on mutual security and human rights.

Before the perestroika period of political restructuring in the Soviet Union began in 1985, early Space Bridges were mostly cultural or musical. "In recent years, we have been able to discuss political issues, and that was a major breakthrough in Soviet and Russian TV," observes Dr. Leonid Zolotarevsky, Director of the Department for International Programming, Russian National State Broadcasting System (Gosteleradio) and Sovtelexport, the self-financed distribution and co-production arm of Soviet television. "It's been a breakthrough in American TV also in that before this time, no one in the U.S. actually saw real Soviet people, the way they look, the way they speak, the way they think."[2]

"For example, our 'Capital Series'—a series of discussions between our parliament, the Supreme Soviet, and the U.S. Congress was produced with ABC News. We got an Emmy award for that series, recognizing that it was important to both the U.S. and U.S.S.R. What's really amazing is that our audience research proved that the audience amounted to 180 to 210 million people at one time.

"Collaborating with Thames Television, we had a most interesting co-production program, with the Soviet and British parliaments joined for 90 minutes in a Space Bridge. It was the first time in its history that the British Parliament was on air.

"We've had that kind of program with many countries—practically with all the west European countries, with Japan, and India—I think perhaps with 20 to 25 countries."[3]

Face-to-face communication through such co-production can have a major impact on world events and individual perceptions. Views of one's enemy, or of the stranger or the immigrant will certainly change as we see each other more frequently and more clearly.

Involving 200 million people in a common debate is remarkable. For the typical citizen who has felt disconnected from the policy decisions that affect his or her life, this Space Bridge means that the views of all sides are debated by those who *actually* make national policy. One can see them. It's the first step toward global democracy. We've moved from a hillside in ancient Greece, where collaboration involved those within earshot, to a global neighborhood, where collaboration can involve all those with television sets. In not too many years, interactive television will enable direct response to the official debates.

In the years ahead, producers of Space Bridge programs will need to overcome new challenges. For example, the topics and formats must be fresh to keep audience interest. Direct feedback and participation must increase yet be manageable and representative of the whole constituency. Economic obstacles must not hinder broadcast. The irony of the situation in the late 80s was that the economically poor Soviet Union was able, because of state ownership of its facilities, to provide ground and satellite services for Space Bridges, but the economically wealthier western countries had difficulty financing their end because of the high cost of commercial television time and the shortage of philanthropic foundation funding for public broadcast time. An extension of the irony is the possibility that the privatization occurring in Russia in the 1990s may hamper or halt these Space Bridges.

Telethons and Teleconferences

Telethons have existed domestically since the 1970s. They are a familiar vehicle for Hollywood fundraising to promote one or another good cause. Just before the Soviet Union collapsed, the Soviets, building on their Space Bridge experiences, sought to use the telethon format for introducing new conversations among people of the world.

A prototype for the first major internationally co-produced telethon was developed in Moscow in 1991. The objective was a non-political focus on veterans of all wars of the 20th century representing all sides of the conflicts. For example, veterans from opposing sides of the Soviet incursions in Hungary, Czechoslovakia and Afghanistan would be included. "We already have some positive responses from United States, Israel, Great Britain, Germany," said Zolotarevsky. "I think there will be 6 to 7 countries participating. It's an entirely new form of co-production."[4]

"We also start work on another telethon for June 1st, 1992—a program on orphans of all countries—not only those who have no parents, but also those who

don't have parents in the form of teachers, tutors for talented kids, etc. This will be an international telethon, initiated by an international fund."[5]

In the coming decade we can expect even more innovation from the Russians. Sovtelexport was created in 1989 as a self-financed international co-production and distribution arm of Gosteleradio. The motivation for this venture is to bring convertible currency into Russia, thereby making possible business that could not be done at that time in rubles. In addition, the Russians want to acquire more updated Western television equipment. Concurrently, more international collaboration and co-production will occur.

Teleconferences, by the late 1980s, became a widely used form of communications, especially in the corporate sector. The form of co-production depends on the nature of the program and its intended audience. Programs to foster communication within a given international organization (or corporation), programs offering classroom-to-classroom experiences for university students, and programs to exchange information between nongovernmental organizations (NGOs) concerned about hunger in Africa are obviously quite different from programs intended for general broadcast. Frequently, however, teleconferences have not involved two-way video. Rather, in order to control costs, sponsors have offered one-way video and two-way audio.

Teleconferencing is a marvelous tool, but technology alone will not enable effective communication if the parties involved have other priorities at the appointed time or if all parties are not fully committed to the event.

For example, a group of television professionals in New York and in Geneva volunteered their time to bring international policy-makers into direct contact with international groups of children, their teachers, and parents to focus on such policy decrees as "Peace Child" and "International Day of Peace." The idea was that the world's leaders would listen to the world's kids—for just a few minutes, once a year. Unfortunately, those world leaders who were expected to participate were late, preoccupied with other commitments, or didn't think that listening to kids was a priority essential to carrying out their jobs. "No one seemed to understand the public relations value of the event," Mary E. Gottemoeller, president of The World Information Corporation and one of the event organizers, observed. "The success of the Reagan administration was derived from their knowing the power of public relations."[6]

As with Space Bridges, collaborative news production and all the other types of co-productions to be discussed, success depends partly on technology (satellites), partly on the management tool (co-production), and mostly on having the participants committed to the reasons for the event.

Teleconferencing opportunities will grow extremely rapidly as the century turns because of the shift in transmission technology from reliance on satellite transmission to fiber optics. Expensive satellite costs will be eliminated. Transmission over telephone lines can occur wherever fiber optic cables exist—wherever telephone lines are easily available. More people can have easy, fairly inexpensive access to teleconferencing technology. Two-way video will be easier and cheaper (see Chapter 4).

Imagine the options for education when experiments like the following can be conducted on a more regular basis. In the early 1980s, Dr. Thomas Naff, Director of the

Middle East Research Institute at the University of Pennsylvania in Philadelphia, involved selected students from U.S. east coast universities in live transmission with students abroad for an hour every 10 days. Those who were involved in the United States were students of either Arabic or Spanish language and culture. Those from abroad were students of English and American culture.[7] Teleconferencing as a form of co-production can make possible a revolution in education. University students and others will be exposed to much of the world heretofore accessible only to the privileged.

Problems remain to be solved, however, before this type of communication is easily usable worldwide. For example, if you were in Bangor, Maine, when would you talk with people in New Zealand? New Zealand is 17 hours ahead of Bangor in time. Another problem is the quantity and quality of telephone lines in the developing countries. It will be some time before such telephone service can equal that in the industrialized countries.

Collaborative News Production

CNN "World Report" plays an important role in allowing journalists worldwide to collaborate in a partnership for international television news production.

Aside from the United States, CNN has an audience of some 55 million TV owners. More than six million people outside the United States receive CNN either via cable or satellite. Unless you live in Greenland or Siberia, CNN is directly available. Before the mid-1990s CNN International will reach an additional eight million European homes by switching its transmission to the Astra 1B Satellite.[8] Others receive CNN through the 120 stations around the world that buy CNN feeds from time to time. Some 250,000 hotel rooms worldwide receive CNN. The global distribution is impressive, but most impressive is the involvement of persons from countries worldwide in program production.

CNN "World Report" started in 1980. Now, 135 to 150 countries contribute 2½-minute pieces each week. "Ted Turner felt there should be a place where broadcasters from all over the world could come together to present the news from their own perspective," comments "World Report" Executive Producer Donna Mastrangelo. "CNN 'World Report' is so special because it's not an American view. In fact, CNN has only one contribution—like any other contributor."[9]

The only prerequisite for being on "World Report" is that one be a broadcaster in one's own country. CNN "World Report" contributors have the right to broadcast the program on their station. At contributor meetings three times a year, CNN may offer help with technical details, but by and large no special training exists for contributors. "As Ted said, 'people have eyes and ears and can learn from each other.' We don't want to Americanize the contributions," explained Mastrangelo.[10] Contributors are responsible for satellite or shipping cost to get their material to CNN Atlanta. Noncontributing stations must contract for the program in the usual manner. CNN holds the worldwide rights. If "World Report" has a great medical piece or a wonderful feature, anyone within the Turner family can use it. In fact, there are times it may be used on another program before it's used on "World Report"—"CNN International" or "Headline News."

"The challenge is to produce international news that viewers see affecting their

lives," says Mastangelo. "I'm still a purist, and I think our main goal is to educate. When I was in the field, the biggest compliment I received was when people said, 'I learned something.' All news can be presented in a way that hits home—personalize it more and that will affect more people. I talk to the contributors. A lot of them ask for ideas. I may say—why don't you key in on one family and tell us about their life—as a way to make your point?"[11]

CNN has only done strict co-productions on selected specials. However, it does co-anchor programs, especially during the time of year when the contributors come together in Atlanta. In the future, it may co-anchor programs on location. For example, a special on Latin America may have a co-anchor from one of the Latin countries. The obstacle, however, is that the broadcaster in Latin America has to handle the satellite costs to get the program back to Atlanta. From Atlanta, the distribution is not a problem.

"I think 'World Report' is the wave of the future," says Mastrangelo. "We've not even begun to tap this opportunity. Business is shrinking: American networks are scaling back and closing bureaus overseas. Now CNN is getting competition from the BBC and new news services in Asia. Competition is good because it will keep us on our toes.

"But, the most important aspect of CNN's 'World Report' is that we have the world at our fingertips. Our contacts are incredible. I know the difference from having worked at another network. I can call almost any country and know someone. We're ahead of the news. Take the Yugoslavian civil war, for example. We reported on it for a long time before others sent journalists in. And during the 1991 Soviet coup that resulted in freedom for the Baltic states, our Lithuanian correspondent called. I transferred him to the studio so he could tell the world what he was telling me: 'They just freed the television station.'"[12]

CO-PRODUCTION IN TRADITIONAL TELEVISION

News Co-Production

The European Broadcasting Union (EBU) is an independent, nonprofit, non-commercial organization that works with other regional broadcasting unions, such as the Arab States Broadcasting Union (ASBU), the Asia-Pacific Broadcasting Union (APBU), the Caribbean Broadcasting Union (CBU), and the former Organization Internationale de Radiodiffusion et Television (OIRT, the EBU equivalent for former Communist bloc countries. It also works with UNESCO, the World Intellectual Property Organization (WIPO), the International Telecommunications Union (ITU), and other international bodies.[13]

"Our particular interest in the EBU is the collaborative gathering and distribution of international news," states Pierre Brunel-Lantenac, Director of the News Study Development and Services section of the EBU. EBU members are all the traditional broadcasters in Europe, including Israel, Turkey, Jordan, and Egypt. "We have included countries that border on the Mediterranean.

"I'm proud that as of January 1991 we have an African exchange—we ex-

changed 92 news items in January and we're learning how to work together. I trained these new partners in our collaboration. At first, it's hard to instill the importance of regular participation, even if you yourself have no news item to offer. One day, the Camaroons had no news, but they sent color bars. This was fantastic. They said they are here with us—partners in the news business. I'm very proud."[14]

Each EBU member has different geography, different needs, and different possibilities. So reciprocity requires goodwill. The EBU offers any news items to any member, and each member provides whatever news she or he can. For example, the EBU used to give OIRT, the Communist equivelent of EBU, nine to ten thousand items per year and would get perhaps four hundred per year, including lots of factory openings and similar items of no international broadcast interest.

Traditionally, the EBU has consisted of public broadcasters; however, in recent times the number of private broadcasters is increasing in Europe and they are joining. The EBU is a coordinating body. It produces nothing itself but it helps members to exchange their news and their current affairs material. It helps them to organize coverage of events like the 1991 war in the Persian Gulf in order to save them money and to solve the problem of satellite capacity. Every year EBU moves twelve to fourteen thousand items. EBU is not a doorkeeper. It just helps the free flow of information. Each chief editor and broadcaster can decide on her or his own commentary.

Lantenac states, "from 4 A.M. Greenwich time to 10 A.M. Greenwich time we are open, and every second something arrives we're ready to exchange the flow of news. Here in Geneva we are go-between technicians to help link newsrooms—not to preempt journalist's decisions. I am a journalist. I understand that it is very dangerous to interfere. Every morning we have a news conference. It is the largest one in the world. In each country we have a news contact—from Dublin to Ankara, from Helsinki to Rabat. Every morning its 'good morning.' It's shared by a news coordinator from one of the offices, working on a rotating basis. For one hour, we discuss the issues of day, what materials are available, who has particular interests or special requests. As soon as there are two requests for the same news item, we distribute it.

"To ensure that the system works, we are in permanent training and refreshment. Twice a year all the people throughout Europe come here to meet with my staff and to study what's happening. Psychologically its fantastic because they all become good friends. For example, on the starting day of the 1973 Yom Kippur War, I called Jerusalem to say it would be hectic and to take care, and the guy there said to me, 'fine, but do you have you any information for me about my friend in Amman? Please, if you speak with Amman tell him my best regards—tell him not to forget he's my friend and if he needs something, to tell people that he's my friend.' Next, I called Amman and my contact there said, 'I have no time to talk, but what about my friend in Jerusalem? We will win, but I will give an order to the King that this man in Jerusalem is my friend and I must protect him.' On this basis, it's possible to do something."[15]

The EBU, like the earlier CNN example, provides a model for international collaboration and co-production of global news—a way to provide a free flow of information, with all countries part of the partnership, to enable each voice and each point of view to be heard in our new global neighborhood.

Sports Co-Production

The ABC/TNT coverage of the 1991 Pan American Games provides a useful model highlighting the opportunities and hurdles in international sports coverage. (Also see Chapter 3 concerning the unusual legal and political problems involved in co-production when one is "trading with the enemy.") Lydia Stephans, Director of Programming for ABC Sports describes the event. "Once we had acquired the rights and had our legal and contractual agreements, we sat with state Cuban television officials—which is a good fraction of the Cuban government because there is no separation between government and broadcasting. We developed a plan of action for producing the games."[16]

Producing the games required decisions about how to get the signal out from a volleyball venue to a broadcast center, where a broadcast center was going to be located, what was needed from the technical side, what was needed from a production side, and what was needed from a personnel side to get the games on television. The schedule for the events had to be synchronized with the telecast schedule. ABC Sports and TNT Sports decided how many hours of Pan-American Games programming they would broadcast. Once the telecast schedule was determined, the next step was to decide which TV entity would get which events. ABC's schedule was basically our "Wide World of Sports" programming hours—4:30–6:00 P.M. Eastern Time every Saturday and 2:00–6:00 P.M. Sunday. TNT designated its available time slots on its cable network. Both networks had commitments to other events and had to stage the Pan-Am games around those programs. Together they had about 90 hours of programming. Network representatives met with the event organizers and identified the events that were particularly important to the American public—basketball, gymnastics, boxing, swimming, diving, track and field—popular events, events in which American athletes were strong and that pull in a strong American TV rating. If it's Mexico vs. Brazil in baseball, most Americans won't stay tuned very long, unless they are avid baseball fans. The networks must be able to show the most appropriate events. ABC and TNT had roundtable discussions with event organizers concerning schedule changes needed to accommodate the television production. The incentive for event organizers to accommodate the television networks was that exposure for the games, the athletes, and resulting high TV ratings could only help those wanting future international games.

Then it was necessary to send representatives to Cuba to look at the venues and to plot where TV cameras would be placed, where production trucks would be parked, where ABC Sports and TNT Sports would set up a broadcast center—a central host studio location where all the signals from all the venues could come back. Brent Musburger, the ABC announcer, needed a place to sit. A broadcast center was needed for the executive producer, the coordinating producer, the directors, and the associate directors, and a place was needed for all the support personnel to be headquartered.

Stephans explained the unique problems of this particular international games."We needed to decide what facilities to bring to Cuba and how to get them there—an enormous task. It was solved when we arranged for a 530-foot cargo ship to carry all our equipment from the coast of Florida to Havana. This included about 8 production trucks (they're semis), about 17 house trailers for office space, about 3 trailers for food, and office supplies (computers, xerox machines, paper, RAID,

paper clips, toilet paper, etc.). Fortunately, Cuba is on the same electrical current as the United States, so we didn't need adapters, but we brought generators, transponders, tape machines, cameras, tape stock. We didn't buy anything in Cuba; we couldn't, because the U.S. government would consider that a violation of the Trading with the Enemy Act.

"The extent of our co-production here was complicated by the political situation. However, we did work with Cuban Television. The way we had set it up was that Cuban Television would be the host broadcaster—i.e., they would supply the TV facilities to the rest of the world. Because they are not as advanced as we are technically, they needed help, which was provided by the Americans and the Canadians. Unlike an Olympics where the host country is the host broadcaster who supplies a clean signal to the rest of the world, ABC Sports and TNT Sports were the host broadcasters. We supplied all the equipment to fill this role for the boxing venue, the basketball venue, the swimming and diving venue. CTV, Canadian Television, supplied all the equipment to be the host broadcaster for the opening ceremonies, track and field, gymnastics, and volleyball. Cuban TV was the host broadcaster for the rest of the events."[17]

Collaboration with Cuban TV meant that ABC and TNT would be given a clean feed from them, that is, video and international sound, and the Americans would supply their own announcers. Cuban TV could take a clean feed from ABC/TNT on the designated events. They weren't allowed to use American announcers, only pictures, and they had to use their own transponders to bring the signal from the venue back to Cuban television.

Other international sports co-productions have differed. For example, in the 1984 Olympics out of Los Angeles, ABC was the host broadcaster and interacted with everyone worldwide. Almost every venue was covered with ABC equipment and personnel, and ABC had people from other countries involved in production and direction. The criteria for deciding where the network could collaborate with television professionals from other countries were really based on communication skills. Network representatives sat down with the appropriate parties, compared styles, and agreed on what product was best in each situation for the particular audience.

Sometimes, network staff travels around the world to produce profiles on athletes with interesting stories or those favored to win. When in Europe, ABC used Carelton TV to provide a British crew. In Moscow, shooting "Challenge of Champions," a figure skating event, ABC worked with Soviet TV. A network relies heavily on the host or the home broadcasters to help. It can't fly everything to another country. If local facilities are sufficient, they are utilized, and some of the local technical people also help.

Networking isn't difficult. ABC has a director of programming in London. He maintains relationships with event organizers and technical people in Europe, so that the U.S. staff knows whom to call. It's also a small world in this regard. People get to know whom to call.

Entertainment Models

Co-production in entertainment is accomplished in a range of ways. This section will examine four models: (1) Radio Television Luxembourg (RTL), a private

station not so much engaged in co-production as in international program segments to satisfy the growing international audience; (2) Grenada, the English-based company that has new projects specifically focused on co-production; (3) West Deutscher Rundfunk (WDR), a large German system struggling with the issues involved in co-production; and (4) the NBC agreement with Mitsui and TV Tokyo to co-venture entertainment programming.

The observation made by Richard Sydenham, producer for the United Nations, is one important to all would-be co-producers: "There's a problem with creative decisions. One person has to be in charge in the end. If the writer is in Canada, and Germans put in the money, and the BBC has the star to be cast—eventually, everyone will tamper with the story and it will become a hodge-podge." [18] Bear this in mind as you examine the various models for collaboration in television entertainment.

Europe's oldest and largest commercial broadcaster, Radio Television Luxembourg (RTL)[19] has pioneered in providing commercial television across borders in Europe. Initially, this was an accident of geography, with the transmitters located in an area of Luxembourg where access to Belgium, France, and West Germany was routine.[20] Today, however, with satellite transmission and the growth of the station, RTL has begun to aggressively seek new audiences across Europe from Spain to Hungary. While the station has bought a lot of American programs, it has also encouraged producers to broaden involvement in the local studio-based productions.

One example of RTL's entertainment programming is the show called "Tieneke," which is aired in early evening on Saturdays. Tieneke de Nooj, the vivacious TV variety show Dutch hostess, has designed her show with a format featuring guests and entertainers filling segments, with discussions of human interest and about current events, demonstration of guests' particular skills, or entertainment. Because the program is now broadcast throughout Europe, it no longer limits itself to Dutch participants (even thought it is produced in the Hilversum studios in the Netherlands). Tieneke brings in persons from the wider program audience. For example, one show included Dutch child poets, a singer from Spain, an entrepreneur who had designed an infrared machine to identify counterfeit bills given to merchants, a lesbian folk singer who was raising a child, and a French cooking segment.[21] The idea was to appeal to an international audience.

Grenada Television, the British independent broadcaster, has escalated its emphasis on international co-production. In 1990, the company decided to build a TV movie division, with emphasis on international co-production. To do this it hired Dighton E. Spooner Jr. as Executive Vice-President of the new Films for Television branch. Grenada needed someone with a sophisticated understanding of how Hollywood worked, someone who knew how programs got made and how networks function, while at the same time having the sensibilities to create things that would work in Europe. Having worked in American public television for 12 years before working for CBS in Hollywood, Spooner was someone able to bridge these gaps.

"With the changes the 1990s are bringing to Europe," says Spooner (see Chapter 3), "there's a great need for European companies to be able to both increase television entertainment production and to find ways to distribute these productions as part of a more continuous flow between Europe and the United States."[22]

There have been clear problems over the years in co-production of entertain-

ment programs. They are best summarized in the disparaging terms "Europudding," and "Mid-Atlantic Programs," that is, programs that meet no one's needs. The consortium of European companies with which Spooner works wants a production arm that will operate with one creative vision. "It is imperative that writers and producers working on co-productions don't have to listen to several different points of view and then worry about satisfying all of them," says Spooner. "So, we have designed a procedure whereby all the companies provide their creative input to me and I communicate to the writers and producers. I bring the ideas to the companies that I think will work. They tell me which ones they like; then I take the material to auction to specific properties, to attach writers to the ideas, or to develop programs to take to the U.S. marketplace. The partners will get the broadcast rights to their programs in their territories as well as a share in the financial obligations and benefits from the program—a share in the income from the program distribution outside their territories."[23]

Spooner described one example of a movie that transcended the "Mid-Atlantic" problem. "It's a story that naturally connects the United States and Europe. It's produced jointly with HBO and called 'Stinger.' An English author wrote the script. It's about an IRA agent sent to the U.S. to illegally buy Stinger missiles to shoot down British helicopters in Northern Ireland. In the U.S. he's opposed by an FBI task force out of New York City designed to stop the inroads of the IRA into the Irish Catholic communities in the northeastern United States. However, the FBI agent's wife is Irish Catholic, and her family are strong supporters of Northern Ireland's independence. He also has to interact with other FBI agents and with N.Y. Police Department people who are Irish sympathizers. It's an antagonistic work environment and a difficult home environment. Its a good story—it bridges the Atlantic. It's entertaining, and it speaks to the nature of relationships and to the things that happen to us as people. It has a common denominator in that it provides a strong invitation to both the American and the European audiences. It may be sited only in one location, but it has a strong enough humanity note that it compels attention from people on both sides of the Atlantic."[24]

Another example is CBS TV working with Grenada to produce as many as six movies in the early 1990s. Similarly, in the late 1980s, Grenada undertook an eight-movie co-production deal with HBO.[25]

West Deutscher Rundfunk (WDR)[26] is West German public television. WDR is one of the regional (Lander) broadcasting corporations that form the Arbeitgemeinschaft der Offentlich-rechtlichen Rundfunkanstalten der Bundesrepublik Deutschland (ARD), the program supplier for radio and for the first and third TV networks.[27] Operating out of Cologne, WDR's principal function is to provide programming for 17 million inhabitants of North-Rhine Westfalia Lander, the largest of the regions within Germany. WDR provides approximately 25% of ARD network programming.[28]

Dr. Annette Wachter, WDR's Director of Strategic Planning, points out that co-production is becoming a measurable percentage of the programming. It's been a rocky road for the overall ARD network. Co-production suffered a setback as the early experiments revealed some of the problems discussed in this chapter. ZDF, The Second German Television Channel, has in the last few years begun to expand its own co-production deals (see Figure 1). Since the early 1980s WDR has had an

German Television Production Trends 1985–1989

Origins of programs (%)

ARD	1985	1986	1987	1988	1989
self-produced	50.80	47.70	48.60	50.30	46.50
co-produced	6.10	5.40	5.90	3.40	4.80
commissioned	4.60	5.40	5.50	6.50	6.30
purchased	14.00	13.50	14.50	17.10	18.20
taken over	4.90	7.40	4.30	5.60	5.30
	100.00	100.00	100.00	100.00	100.00
repeats	19.60	20.90	21.20	18.40	18.90

Source: ARD Jahrbücher 1986–1990

Origins of programs (%)

ZDF	1985	1986	1987	1988	1989
self-produced	48.70	49.50	49.10	51.80	49.80
co-produced	1.50	2.70	1.60	1.80	2.00
commissioned	17.50	17.00	16.30	14.60	16.30
purchased	29.40	28.20	28.50	29.90	28.90
taken over	2.90	2.60	4.50	1.90	3.00
	100.00	100.00	100.00	100.00	100.00
repeats	18.00	28.90	19.40	19.80	22.00

Source: ZDF Jahrbücher 1985–1989

▶ *Figure 1*   *German Television: Production Trends 1985–1989.*

in-house staff focused on marketing and international co-production. WDR works hard to ensure that its co-productions are appropriate. It is particularly aware of the many potential difficulties. For example, something as simple as a German soap opera is very different from a French soap opera, and they can't be interchanged.[29]

Dr. Manfred Jenke, WDR Director of Broadcasting, further illustrated the problem producers face in developing co-production scripts. "I saw a German/Italian/French co-production. It involved three hour-long programs. A German girl went to Italy and met a young Italian. They fell in love. But the daughter of a French banker, who was more attractive than the German girl, eventually ended up with the Italian boy. That was very synthetic. It's what they call 'Europudding.' It won't work. To construct a plot that should appeal to all three publics is too artificial. I think the European Media '92 people have realized that in the European Community we must still provide for genuine national products, then sell them to the national retail cinema organizations in a wider market."[30]

Jenke points out that entertainment co-production must involve thoughful script writing if it is to be successful. He asks, "does international co-production carry an implicit mandate for programming to improve international understanding?

If so, consider the possibility that a real *national* production might offer a better international understanding of a particular culture and its people.

"For example," Jenke observes, "the 10th showing of 'Gone with the Wind' on German Television on the eve of the 1991 Persian Gulf War did much more to make people in Europe aware of what was going on with the American military in Kuwait and Iraq than any co-production one could imagine."[31]

By the early 1990s the international market had begun to overcome the problems cited by WDR. By the 1991 International Film and Program Market for Television, Video, Cable and Satellite (Marché International des Films et des Programmes pour la Télévision, la Vidéo, le Câble et le Satellite—MIPCOM) Festival, U.S. cable networks were actively sealing co-production deals. The Arts & Entertainment Network (A&E) produced "Spies" with CBS and Columbia House. Showtime signed several deals, including "Palio" produced with Itel and Reteitalia, and "Darkside" with BBC and Canal Plus. Nickelodeon signed a deal to co-produce an animated series "Doug" with Elipse and to develop Elipse's "Mot." USA Network signed co-productions with Italy's Quinta and with British Lion.[32]

The Japanese approach to collaborative entertainment programming is primarily through co-ventures. In 1990 an agreement was signed whereby through NBC-Mitsui/TV Tokyo will distribute NBC entertainment programs in Japan, co-produce television shows, and acquire the distribution rights for movies and other programs in Japan and perhaps in neighboring Asian markets. Beyond these three agreements, the partners will jointly explore new investments—especially the creation of new channels in Japan. The co-venture is to be managed through a new office called NNBC established in 1991 in Tokyo.[33]

Japan's Mitsubishi and Westinghouse Broadcasting International announced a production/distribution agreement in early 1992 whereby Mitsubishi will be the exclusive representative for Westinghouse's program catalogue in Japan. Long term, they anticipate co-production for worldwide distribution and for high-definition television.[34]

Documentary Co-Productions

PBS, the American Public Broadcasting System, has been one of the pioneers in co-production. As the saying goes, "necessity is the mother of invention." Scarce production resources, a chronic problem for public television in America, gave birth to co-production. One of the jewels in the PBS crown is the science documentary "Nova." "Nova" makes 20 new programs a year, of which 10 arrive in some form from other producers—an uncompleted film, an idea with funding from external sources, or a completed film.

Director of Acquisitions Alain Jehlan, explains "Nova"'s approach to co-production. "Some of our 20 programs are nominal co-productions like the ones really made by the BBC series called "Horizons." We buy at least three, sometimes five, of those per year. They are nominal because "Horizon" makes them, and our input comes in the form of comments. Other films are more genuine co-productions where we work with people along the way to shape the program. For example, we are making a film on the reintroduction into the wilderness of the California condor, a bird which is almost extinct. Scientists captured all of them because they didn't think they could keep them alive in the wild. Now they are beginning to reintroduce

them in California. When that's done they will reintroduce them elsewhere because in California they probably can't live. The film is made by a French producer who had before made a film on vultures. He is making it from his point of view—mostly photographing the Andes. Because we're interested in the California end, a producer from 'Nova' went to California to work with him to be sure he got the California footage that fit the 'Nova' style. Our style is different from that of most other scientific documentary series. We have a lot more science—more content. That program is a genuine co-production."[35]

The French filmmaker with whom "Nova" worked is an independent producer and director. He works with a small company consisting of a stable of independents in France. There are two understandings of the term *producer* in France. This filmmaker is a *realizateur/auteur*, that is, a producer/author who works in the field rather than *producteur*, the producer who puts together the financing for the project. The company he's affiliated with puts together the deals. He's really a prominent scientist who also makes films.

"Co-productions are a bigger and bigger piece of our business," says Jehlan. "In the past more films came to us already completed. But now, people are having a harder and harder time getting funds to complete documentary films or videos. They need what's called a *presale*—on our side that's called a *co-production*. In this deal we would provide financing and supervision and hope they would do the finishing work to result in a production suitable for inclusion in our particular television series. The terms of presales and co-productions vary depending on the individual situation. We almost always do the narration. We certainly direct the narration right here—at our WGBH Boston headquarters. We need a constant format. We also do the packaging—i.e., our openings and credits."[36]

Other examples of "Nova" co-productions include a project with Film Australia on Chinese history. The model was similar to that used with the French filmmaker; however, someone at WGBH who knows Chinese history was involved in the script writing and in the shoots.

The Christian Science Monitor and USSR State Television began an interesting co-production in 1991. Dr. Leonid Zolotarevsky, now Director of the Department of International Programming for the Russian National State Broadcasting Company describes it. "It is a one-hour prime time program shown weekly on the Monitor channel. The program is called 'Rodina' which is Russian for *motherland*—a name given by our colleagues, not ourselves. We supply 60 minutes of tape every week on every aspect of life in the former Soviet Republics—now The Commonwealth of Independent States. It's 100% unbiased and a nonpolitical program. We include all kinds of stories based not just in Moscow but across the country. We supply Monitor Television with the story and commentary in Russian. They translate it and put on a voice-over. They do the electronic effects—the polish work—through their Moscow bureau."[37]

Issue programs such as "One World Week" was a co-production that occurred in May 1990 in Europe. It involved a full week focusing on environmental projects. Seven countries and various public television stations were involved. Everyone had a different view of what the program would be; the Germans favored all discussion, the Portuguese and the Scandinavians wanted other formats. The co-producers decided that a percentage of the programming would be mutual and then stations

could pick and choose from the remaining productions what they would play. Each station would play and produce some of it itself. The One World Broadcasting Trust, based in London, played a major role in spearheading the event. This organization exists to increase understanding between the developed and the developing worlds.[38]

Educational Co-Productions

Educational television differs from documentaries produced for broadcast in that the objective is to reach an audience of students: young people, those perfecting their professional skills, or those focused on working with specific institutions. Co-production here has enormous potential. Information is shared, professional production staff is shared, and costs are cut. Those for whom the programming is produced are educated about the value of collaboration in their own careers. Two models will be discussed: the United Nations and the Educational Broadcasting Trust in London.

United Nations programs are largely institutional TV. According to Richard Sydenham, U.N. producer, "it's not easy to get educational programs onto broadcast TV in the U.S. because there's so much programming already available. It's different in the countries of Africa and Asia; there's less entertainment program competition. Primarily, however, U.N. productions are designed for high school and college audiences. The productions work with general audiences, but often a young person presents the topic to draw the attention of younger people. Because the issues the United Nations covers can be dense and complicated, we usually do an educational study guide to go with a video cassette."[39]

U.N. co-productions range in substance from Mickey Mouse's 60th birthday party to programs on apartheid, Palestine, African decolonization, literacy, the environment, development, and human rights, with an emphasis on children's rights. Many of these productions are educational videos of 15–20 minutes.

Sydenham adds, "We did a half-hour documentary titled 'About the United Nations: Literacy.' It focuses on literacy for women. It comes with a teacher's manual titled 'Teaching about Literacy' and is intended for use with high school students in civics, social studies, history, and geography classes. This project was a good example of collaboration among the U.N. agencies. We'd been approached by the U.N. Development Fund for Women, who wanted to put up some money for a production on this topic. The Special Programs Section of the Department of Public Information then found funding from seven other U.N. agencies interested in these issues, the U.N. Fund for Population, WHO, UNICEF, the International Labor Organization, the Division for Women in Vienna, and the Department of Public Information."[40]

Sydenham's office produced the program. Commenting on the production, Sydenham notes, "I wanted a uniform look, with original tape and not stock footage. So I used a production company here in New York who could both shoot and edit. I wanted to edit here in New York. I knew their work was very good. We were allowed considerable editorial freedom although the United Nations Development Fund for Women (UNIFEM) had the final say at the point of script approval, rough cut, etc. All the partners got masters and can make their own distribution copies for their own use. We'll also distribute it in three languages to U.N. Information Centers. We did not have a special mandate from the General Assembly for the literacy project, although it did tie in with the International Year for Women. Our budget was not

large, but it was enough to do some original filming. We ended up filming in Mali, Thailand, Costa Rica, and New York. The company we hired took its own crew abroad. I calculated the cost options and found the deal that they gave us was advantageous to us. I was able to use a crew I had already worked with; I knew the photographer's abilities. The photographer was actually the editor. We also collaborated with UNICEF, who had a crew available to do a week of shooting for us in Thailand."[41]

The United Nations also has a production unit in Geneva, an outpost of the New York office. The political headquarters of the United Nations does things differently from the member agencies. Those agencies—UNICEF, UNESCO in Paris, the International Labor Organization (ILO), the World Health Organization (WHO), the U.N. High Commission for Refugees—have an in-house news or documentary production capacity of their own. They work on very specific assignments. The productions authorized from the U.N. political headquarters cover much broader topics. It may use existing agency footage or produce its own.

Skill Banks like the Educational Broadcasting Services Trust (EBS), a trust with charitable status for education and training based in the United Kingdom, offer another unique educational service. EBS started as an offshoot of the BBC to secure funds aside from the BBC license fee that could go into educational projects. The BBC has a long history of experimenting in international co-productions and of exploring other innovative ventures. Jim Stevenson, EBS Chief Executive and former head of the BBC Education Department, describes this innovative approach to the co-production of educational video.[42] "This approach is part of the 1980s privatization efforts."

"The BBC contracts with us for programs. They give us funds. We hire an outside producer, and we handle the legal and financial work and retain editorial control. EBS has range of projects. Our largest is the Skill Bank. It's a bank of video modules which will accumulate over five years to teach simple skills in the workplace from plumbing and pipe bending to the care of old people. This is a semi-commercial venture. It's co-production in the sense that EBS works with 47 colleges who have each put in £5000 to fund the programs. Often they also contribute expertise to the production. We make the programs. We give them to the colleges to distribute as they wish. Programs are not very long. Some are only 9 minutes. One is 30 minutes. We sell them. We aim to do 200 in five years. This year we'll make 25. We have an agent here who is now our distributor, and he has exclusive rights for the whole world. While we've started in England, we intend to work with others throughout the world on the project. So we'll do them in other languages. By and large they are culture free—not very British. Occasionally we run into specific practices that require special attention, such as cutting meat is done differently by butchers in France than it is by English butchers."

While EBS is just beginning the internationalization of its co-production, it serves as a useful model from the perspective that to operate the skill bank, EBS must operate with legal agreements with 47 colleges and another with 15 local education authorities with whom they co-produce one product.

"On educational projects it's nearly impossible to make a profit—even recover funds—production costs are so high and you can never sell at high enough rate,"

says Stevenson. "You need someone to subsidize the project. A sponsor's incentive may be that it wants its name on it or because they are a government agency charged to undertake this service. The incentive for subsidy increases when the cost/benefit ratio is high. For example, the college consortium could never make a product for £5000. And when they have this product, each member school can make money by renting it or selling it. The £5000 per year is well spent.

"Another value in the EBS model is that it is not production for transmission. Now is the time to explore modular video. We're getting further away from transmission—either on open air or cable or satellite. I really believe less and less of that as a delivery mode. When you can copy a video cassette for a pound, then why pay enormous transmission costs, especially for a small audience—and all our stuff is only for a small audience. Broadcasters have tried to deal with the small audience matter. Here, BBC Select provides a viewer a black box to descramble specialized programs. But, it costs £7000 per hour just to transmit. You can make a lot of video cassettes for that. Who out there is going to buy a black box and pay for the program in the night when they can go down the road and get it in a shop? The producers never did their sums."[43]

Corporate TV

International corporate television is big business, producing and frequently co-producing a wide range of productions: training tapes, company Chief Executive Officer (CEO) statements that must reach many people at same time for political reasons, staff conferences, the premarketing introduction of new equipment, and the explanation of new software or new products.

Three examples will be discussed here:

1. A producer in New York has a contract with a Chinese textile company with plants in West Africa and elsewhere around world. She'll develop management training tapes. Among the issues posed by this project is the problem of how to handle cross-cultural management styles for Chinese in Nigeria. "Global corporate management is key in the next few years", says Mary E. Gottermoeller, President, The World Information Corporation. "This will involve computer simulations and models as well as video. Models of American management don't transfer successfully to Western Europe. Why should they transfer to rest of the world?"[44]

2. Corporate video production units around the world allow companies like Hewlett Packard to launch a product in California and announce it to its whole international network all at once. This has been difficult for people because you have to use so many different satellites to reach the proper locations. It's been complicated and time consuming to get into Europe because everything has been country controlled. As the European Community becomes a reality, bureaucracy in Europe should become less cumbersome.[45] At the beginning of the 1990s fiber optic teleconferencing became a reality. This technology will greatly increase teleconference flexibility (see Chapter 4).

3. A multi-national corporation may co-produce for program delivery purposes. For example, one company headquartered in Paris did a series of programs on its product and wanted to use them in the United Kingdom. They'd have to be dubbed in English, so in the end they decided to do a co-production of a program rather than a production. One factor that limits corporate enthusiasm about co-productions on a grand scale is proprietary concerns of private entrepreneurs in a field of competitors. "They're very secretive—even paranoid about not wanting their material circulated," says Tony Goodman, Deputy Director of IVCA, the international professional association for those working in corporate visual communications.[46]

As is evident from the models described in this chapter, there are many ways to approach international television collaboration and co-production. The interested professional can produce many types of products and can work for many different institutions. In addition, one can do one's own productions, offering them to the market through contacts like those described in this chapter and in later chapters. Subsequent chapters explore some of the challenges to be faced by independent producers. As television markets change, new opportunities for co-production emerge. Ventures described in this chapter that are more collaboration than co-productions today may well become co-productions tomorrow. The principal limit to the possibilities for a new producer comes when one's imagination is restricted.

Notes

1. Michael, Brainerd, "Linking the Superpowers through Space Bridges," USA-USSR Media Studies Conference (New York: Gannett Foundation Media Center, Columbia University, New York, 1991), p. 26.
2. Personal interview with Dr. Leonid A. Zolotarevsky, Director, Department for International Programming, U.S.S.R. National State Broadcasting Company, Moscow, Russia, June 13, 1991.
3. Ibid.
4. Ibid.
5. Ibid.
6. Personal interview with Mary E. (Meg) Gottemoeller, President, World Information Corporation, 501 East 17th Street, Flatbush, Brooklyn, NY, tel.: 718-282-8027, December 16, 1990.
7. Contact the Middle East Research Institute, University of Pennsylvania, Philadelphia, PA 19104, tel.: 214-243-6078.
8. Michael Schwelein, "CNN: Television for the Global Village," *World Press Review*, (The Stanley Foundation, 200 Madison Ave., New York, NY 10016, tel.: 212-889-5155), December 1990, p. 34. Also see Meredith Amdur, "Shrinking Budgets Make for Smaller World," *Broadcasting*, Vol. 122, No. 17, April 20, 1992, p. 39.
9. Telephone interview with Donna Mastrangelo, Executive Producer, "CNN World Report," 1 CNN Center, 7th Floor, North Tower, Atlanta, GA 30303, November 6, 1991.
10. Ibid.
11. Ibid.

12. Ibid.

13. Catalogue of Publications (European Broadcasting Union, Ancienne Route 17a/Casa Postale 67, CH-1218 Grand Saconnex, Geneva, Switzerland), February 1990.

14. Personal interview with Pierre Brunel-Lantenac, Director, News Operations, European Broadcasting Union, Ancienne Route 17a/Casa Postale 67, CH-1218 Grand Saconnex, Geneva, Switzerland, Fax: 022-798-5897, tel.: 022-717-2821, February 22, 1991.

15. Ibid.

16. Personal interview with Lydia Stephans, Director, Programming, ABC Sports, 47 West 66th Street, New York, NY 10023, tel.: 212-456-3702, August 23, 1991.

17. Ibid.

18. Personal interview with Richard Sydenham, Producer, Special Programs Section, Department of Information, United Nations, Room S-955, New York, NY 10017, Fax: 212-963-4556, tel.: 212-963-6944.

19. Compagnie Luxembourgeoise de Telediffusion (CLT) owns RTL. RTL, Villa Louvigny, 2850 Luxembourg, tel.: 352-47-66-1, Fax: 352-47-66-27-30.

20. Sidney W. Head, World Broadcasting Systems: A Comparative Analysis (Belmont, California: Wadsworth, 1985), p. 379.

21. Personal interview with Tieneke de Nooj, Producer, RTL Studios, Hilversum, The Netherlands, March 2, 1991.

22. Personal interview with Dighton E. Spooner, Jr., Executive Vice President, Films for Television, Grenada Television, 36 Golden Square, London W1R 4AH, England, fax: 213-282-8992, tel.: 213-282-8996, February 15, 1991.

23. Ibid.

24. Ibid.

25. "CBS to Co-Produce with Grenada," *Broadcasting,* Vol. 119, No. 23, December 3, 1990, p. 62.

26. WDR, Appelhofplatz 1, 5000 Koln 1, Germany, tel.:49-221-22-01, fax: 49-221-220-480/3884.

27. "Public Radio and Television in the Federal Republic of Germany" (Frankfurt am Main: Hessischer Rundfunk, Bertramstrasse 8, D-6000 Frankfurt am Main 1, Germany), April 1985.

28. Ibid. Also see Head, p. 152.

29. Personal interview with Dr. Annette Wachter, Director of Strategic Planning, West Deutscher Rundfunk, Appellhofplatz 1, Postfach 10 19 50, 5000 Koln 1, Germany, fax: 49-221-220-3539, tel.: 49-221-220-4140, February 27, 1991.

30. Personal interview with Dr. Manfred Jenke, Director of Broadcasting, Westdeutscher Rundfunk, Appellhofplatz 1, Postfach 10 19 50, 5000 Koln, Germany, fax: 49-221-220-3539, tel.: 49-221-220-4140, February 27, 1991.

31. Ibid.

32. "Cable's MIPCOM Presence," *Broadcasting,* Vol. 121, No. 17, October 21, 1991, pp. 43–44.

33. "NBC Signs Two Deals with Japanese Firms," *Broadcasting,* Vol. 119, No. 26, December 24, 1990, p. 14.

34. Meredith Amdur, European Correspondent, "Dealing in Monte Carlo," *Broadcasting,* Vol. 122, No. 8, February 17, 1992, p. 31.

35. Personal interview with Alain Jehlan, Director of Acquisitions, "Nova," WGBH, Boston, August 27, 1991.

36. Ibid.

37. Zolotarevsky interview.

38. Gottemoeller interview.

39. Sydenham interview.

40. Ibid.

41. Ibid.

42. Personal interview with Jim Stevenson, Chief Executive, Educational Broadcasting Services Trust, 1/2 Marylebone High Street, London W1A 1AR, England, fax: 01-224-2426, tel.: 01-927-5023, February 15, 1991.

43. Ibid.

44. Gottemoeller interview.

45. Ibid.

46. Personal interview with Tony Goodman, Deputy Director, IVCA, Bolsover House, 5/6 Clipstone St., London W1P 7EB, England, February 15, 1991.

3

▼
▼
▼ **Legal, Political, and**
▼ **Economic Realities**
▼

What actually happens, or doesn't happen, in co-production is greatly affected by laws and regulations, political situations, and economics. If you are working on co-production for a large institution—a TV network, a major production house, or a government agency—principal legal and political issues will be handled by appropriate departments within the organization, and you may need to pay less attention to them. But if you are an independent producer on contract to an institution, operating your own production company, or working free-lance, you will have to cope directly with these issues. While the specifics of dealing with legal and political issues change constantly, some key approaches may be applied in almost all situations.

LAWS, REGULATIONS, AND CONTRACTS

Many creative artists and producers think laws and regulations need to understood only by politicians and lawyers. While the underlying legal and regulatory structure covering frequency allocation, transmission, and station ownership and management are, indeed, mandated by politicians and interpreted and dealt with by lawyers, the producer must deal with the realities stemming from these edicts. Let's look at those most frequently occurring.

Copyright Law

The issue of protecting ownership of creative work is a complicated one in this era of new technologies; it becomes even more complex when dealing with international co-production. Laws that exist in one country may be enforceable in that country—but not in another country. Don't expect U.S. law to function everywhere.

International copyright protections can be found in the 1952 Universal Copyright Convention sponsored through the United Nations Educational, Scientific, and Cultural Organization (UNESCO). This convention updated the 1887 Berne Convention for the Protection of Literary and Artistic Works—the first international copyright convention. The United States and the Soviet Union had not signed the 1887 document. The 1952 convention was designed to make available educational materials for developing countries at less cost. While compliance differs from one country to another, major progress occurred in giving "authors, composers, publishers, producers and others the right to prevent performance of their work without license and payment of royalties."[1]

In recent decades, an increasing number of countries have upheld the Copyright Convention, particularly when expressed in traditional forms. New technologies, however, have complicated the matter of copyright enforcement. For example, the U.S. Copyright Law of 1976 introduced a "retransmission rights concept," allowing copyright holders to demand extra payment for materials delivered via satellite or cable to markets not covered by the original rights purchased by the broadcaster. Worldwide syndication creates enforcement problems because the laws in each country are different.[2] None of the changes in the law have protected the artist's material from VCR tape piracy that has become common in developing countries.

For more information about the United States Copyright Act of 1976 (Public Law [PL]94-553, 90 Stat 2541), the new law that supercedes the Act of 1909 as amended, contact the U.S. Copyright Office.[3]

A U.S. Law—Trading with the Enemy Act

A recent example of the importance of laws with which a co-producer might need to deal is the television broadcast of the 1991 Pan American Games held in Cuba. The 1991 Pan American Games broadcast was a joint venture between ABC sports and TNT sports (a Turner property). ABC sports was the network broadcaster and TNT sports was its cable partner. It was one of the first major international joint ventures where a network and a cable property, not related in any way, shape, or form, together covered the same event.

ABC sports negotiated for the American rights to the event with the help of Transworld International, which is the TV branch of International Management Group, and with the Cuban and Pan American organizing body. "But before the event could take place, ABC sued the U.S. government. The Treasury Department, on behalf of the U.S. government, had stated that ABC and TNT could not carry out the project because they would be in violation of the 'Trading with the Enemy Act.' Cuba was classified as an enemy of the United States," stated Lydia Stephans, Director of Programming, ABC sports.[4] "The basis for the ABC lawsuit was that it violated the United States Constitution's First Amendment rights by denying the American public the right to see the events in which American athletes were competing."[5]

ABC ended up settling out of court with the government. It reached an agreement that ABC sports would have a licensing agreement with the U.S. Treasury Department. This agreement stipulated all the details of business transactions for the Pan American Games.

"According to the 'Trading with the Enemy Act,' Americans are not able to engage in any business transactions with the Cubans. By our paying a rights fee, paying for hotels, etc., we were doing business with the Cubans. So we ended up not paying a rights fee and being limited to a specific amount of money that we could spend while we were there. It was stipulated in our licensing agreement which we followed just to the 'T,'" Stephans noted.

"ABC and TNT together took 330 staff to Cuba, including our on-air personalities, our production, management, and engineering staffs—only the skeleton crew that would be needed to make sure that we could put on a first class event. This was

probably one-third the size group we took to the Olympics in Calgary, Canada, or to Sarajevo, Yugoslavia, to put on the Olympics. We stripped to the bare minimum.

"What pulled the strings more than anything else was the licensing agreement with the American government. I think if there were no politics involved and we hadn't had to abide by a licensing agreement, we probably would have come in there and set up something technically easier, but we wouldn't have been as involved with the Cubans. We had to rely on Cuban technology in order not to pay."[6]

European Community Law

The Single European Act was signed in 1986 by the heads of state of each member of the European Community (EC) (Belgium, Denmark, Germany, France, Greece, Ireland, Italy, Luxembourg, the Netherlands, Portugal, Spain, and the United Kingdom). After ratification by national Parliaments, it became law in July 1987.[7] Decisions about communications policy followed as Europe prepared for the 1992 reality of a single economic market.

The EC Directive Concerning the Pursuit of Television Broadcasting Activities was adopted by the EC Council of Ministers in Luxembourg on October 3, 1989. One objective in this Directive was to call upon member states to ensure that the majority of broadcast programming is of European origin. Such European works are defined to include programming originating from member states or from other European states which are party to the convention, which also meet one of three conditions (1) productions made by producers "established" in member states, (2) productions supervised and controlled by producers in member states, (3) productions where a majority of financing is provided by EC co-producers and co-production is not controlled by producers established outside the EC.[8]

The American motion picture industry mobilized considerable opposition to the Directive, and legal, economic, and diplomatic posturing has followed. On the one hand, according to testimony presented to hearings before the U.S. House Committee on Energy and Commerce, Subcommittee on Telecommunications and Finances,[9] export of U.S. television programming and film is the second largest contributor to a positive trade balance for the United States, returning more than $2.5 billion to the United States during 1988. Of this total, $1.8 billion came from Europe alone. Some members of the American industry found the new EC Directive threatening.

On the other hand, according to Fred Cate, "a virtual explosion in European broadcasting outlets is expected to increase available air time in EC countries from 250,000 hours per year to more than 400,000 hours per year within five years. And, under present regulations, only 14% of United Kingdom broadcasts are U.S. programs. The non-European broadcasting in the rest of Europe is 23%. Consequently, with the increased air time available, the potential for growth is enormous."[10] As summarized by the Trans-Atlantic Dialogue on European Broadcasting, consisting of U.S. and European industry officials including those from NBC, CBS, Capital Cities/ABC Video Enterprises, Fox, the Hearst Corporation, Warner Brothers, and Walt Disney Television, "Some television professionals believe that the Directive also provides substantial new opportunities for non-European investors to play a

vital role in the rapid expansion of the European production industry, making programs in Europe using European talent."[11]

On the other side of the coin, Europeans know that the United States has citizenship laws restricting ownership of U.S. broadcast outlets, and that the United States imports less than 2% of its broadcast programming.[12]

The legal changes in Europe have certainly stimulated activity and controversy. Increased co-production will be one result of the new structure for the media.

Focusing the Directive on an EC member state and its public station, WDR in Cologne, Manfred Jenke, WDR Director of Broadcasting, observed that "WDR makes a lot of productions themselves so the 1992 realization of a single European Economic Community will not affect WDR so much. ARD, the primary German television network of which WDR is part, now produces more than 50% of its own programming. ZDF, the second German channel, is slightly different. They buy a lot and have a lot of co-production. They have built up a European co-production association with other broadcasting companies. The EC authorities in Brussels found great pressure in trying to bar American products, so their 'Media 92' program emphasizes encouraging European production."[13]

Jenke questions the value of enforcing quotas that exclude supposedly excessive American programming. "If the limits present problems for a station, the station will buy only the most appealing items—the soaps, 'Dallas,' etc. There'll be no space left for the best U.S. programs on culture."

British-based Granada Television provides another view of the EC laws and the 1992 economic market changes. Granada has partners in a European consortium with the objectives of reversing the flow of programs from the United States to Europe and rather to increase supply from Europe to the United States. Such activity has developed increased momentum in the 1990s.

Dighton Spooner, Granada's Executive Vice President of Films for Television, doesn't see major changes immediately. "Companies have been co-producing programs within Europe and with American broadcasters for a long time. When I worked at WGBH in Boston we co-produced programs over a decade ago with ZDF in Germany and with the French. With ZDF we did 'Evening at Pops.' Antenne 2 in France was part of co-production on 'Vietnam: A Television History.' Central TV in London was part of that too. We did things with the Japanese. American public television has been doing co-productions for a long time. The reasons now are the same as in the past—a common creative vision and a desire to do things together that are more difficult financially or creatively to do separately. The difference now is that commercial television is feeling the economic pressures that have been commonplace in American public television for a decade."[14]

Nonetheless, changes in business practices are inevitable in the 1990s. Part of this change will be a considerable increase in the number of co-productions. Because of the size of the American commercial industry and its worldwide impact, economic variables within the American industry are bound to have a ripple effect in other countries. Because of the proliferation of private stations competing with the traditional public stations in Europe and elsewhere, the pressure is great for increased programming—programming that can draw audience interest. The legal form provided by the European Community Directive may simply channel these

changes so that Europe's television market develops as a model for the rest of the world of the 21st century (except perhaps for the United States, which is already in a unique position).

For co-producers working in Europe, the legal section of the Independent Program Producers Association (IPPA) book *Co-Production* provides a good introduction to specific applicable national laws.[15]

Treaties

In some countries, where government either owns television or worries about quotas or subsidies, actual treaties have been signed to spell out collaboration between the governments in co-production of films and videos. England is a leading example of a country that has developed such treaties. United Kingdom treaties exist with Italy, Germany, Norway, Canada, Australia, and New Zealand. To learn more about how British co-producers can collaborate with treaty partners, contact the Films Branch of the Department of Trade and Industry in London.[16]

France, the Netherlands, Belgium, Spain, and Germany have signed similar treaties, each with a separate set of countries.[17] It is important to note, however, that the treaties do not interfere with ad hoc co-production arrangements that are made all the time. The treaty simply might help secure resources.

Regulatory Agencies

Throughout the world, nations have established regulatory agencies charged with the job of interpreting and enforcing the laws that have been made. By and large the individual involved in co-production is not the person directly dealing with regulatory matters: this task usually rests with corporate management.

Nonetheless, one should be aware of these agencies and how they might affect the work of a co-producer. In the United States the Federal Communications Commission (FCC) is the principal regulatory agency. It is prevented by the Communications Act of 1934 from directly censoring any subject matter. But the same Act gives the FCC the prerogative of taking action against stations that broadcast materials it deems obscene. The definitions are, of course, subjective. The co-producer's major concern in the area of obscenity is to be aware that different standards for definitions of obscene exist in parts of Europe than in the United States. For example, something co-produced with the French or Italians might play very well in France or Italy, but in the United States it might be considered obscene.

On the other hand, the Australian Broadcasting Tribunal, Australia's regulatory agency can ban specific programs that don't meet its standards.[18] The Israel Broadcasting Authority (IAB) has a mandate as an independent regulatory agency to ensure that the broadcasting system is an "instrument for forging a new state and society." Controversy has occurred over Palestinian-oriented programs.[19]

In general, regulatory concerns, other than political, relate principally to issues of sex, violence, religion, and sometimes native language. In the late 1970s Brazil censored soap operas, requiring that each soap have a certificate of approval before it could be broadcast. It was forbidden to address political, religious, sexual, racial, or economic themes in the scripts. Developing countries have sometimes censored entertainment and news that they believe is contrary to the state welfare.[20]

Another regulatory restriction on producers is called *prior restraint*—the American legal term for censoring something before the fact. This is not done by the regulatory agency but by whoever is in a position to interfere with press freedoms. For example, in the 1991 Persian Gulf War, the U.S. Department of Defense contributed to prior restraint of journalists' work in a wide range of ways.

John Fialka, Defense Correspondent for the *Wall Street Journal,* observed that in the U.S. Civil War, more than a century ago, it took one day to get the news from the Battle of Bull Run to New York City. In 1991, despite instant satellite telephone capabilities, it took three days to get news from Kuwait to New York City because of editorial inaction on the part of the Defense Department team determining whether the news would violate security. He also noted that while photographers produced some 6000 frames per day of the war, only 20 were released each day. Reporters were encouraged to cover the high-tech equipment for which the Defense Department sought continued congressional appropriations; they were given little opportunity to cover the conventional weapons and the troops that were actually responsible for most of the military action. This form of censorship was one of interfering with news coverage in order to turn it into public relations for the U.S. Defense Department.[21]

The type of censorship practiced by the military during the war can be categorized as (1) delaying copy, that is, not allowing journalists to file their stories in a timely fashion; (2) denying access, that is, preventing access to critical battle areas contrary to the practice in prior wars; and (3) controlling electronic access, that is, access to satellite resources for transmitting material to one's newspaper or station.[22]

Customs Regulations

"Even without translation, it was plain to see that our luggage was not moving through the conveyor," observed Harry Mums, President of Paramax Productions, Inc. of Venice, California.[23] He was on his way to produce a tape with people in the Soviet Union.

Unless the equipment gets through customs, in both directions, international co-production will be next to impossible. Traveling internationally as a co-producer of a program, you don't want to find yourself at a shoot hundreds of miles from the port of entry, waiting a week for your equipment to clear customs.

Independent filmmaker Herb Fuller notes, "Trying to understand the natural flow of customs of a particular country is very important advance work. The basis of getting through customs is to promise to bring your equipment back when you leave the country. If it's stolen, it's 'imported' and you have to pay the tariff. To avoid tariff payments and to expedite crossing national borders, make a list of your luggage items before going through customs so that if the officials want to see all your camera filters you know how many there are and where they are. It's also important to know what the valuation information is beforehand and to carry proof of purchase for particularly expensive items.

"Little things can become problems. For example, getting film developed can be an issue. If you send it out ahead, then you will take out less than you brought in. If you want to send it out and get it back, assuming an incredibly efficient transportation network, you must find the right forms for the bureaucracy to process.

These matters, though time consuming, are fairly routine in the industrialized democracies, but they can prove much more difficult in developing countries.[24]

Fuller emphasized the importance of being prepared for the bureaucracy and the time delays caused by customs. "In Portugal, packages come into customs around the clock, but they only leave during a narrow window of the customary work day. No one can get around this. At a shoot on the island of Madeira, we were on furthest outpost of empire—600 miles southwest of Lisbon, off the coast of Africa. We had equipment at the Lisbon airport held for customs. Perhaps we should have hired one of the customs brokers listed in the telephone directory, but I'm not sure it would have been any faster."[25]

Contracts

Every co-production relies heavily on the specific legal contract drawn up between the participating parties for each particular production. Even the smallest company or independent producer must do business through contracts—production contracts, distribution contracts, contracts to purchase rights. The contract determines roles, responsibilities, benefits, and costs associated with undertaking a specific project.

Richard Sydenham, U.N. producer, suggested to those interested in international co-production that "a partnership can sometimes be more serious than a marriage. Marriages may be easier to dissolve."[26] In deciding what to include in a contract, think through every step of the production process and decide how to allocate the decisionmaking powers, how to allocate the distribution of costs and remuneration, and how disputes—if they arise—will be resolved. Sydenham's list of items that one should clearly define in a production contract includes:

1. the name of the partnership and who members are;
2. the scope of the business to be undertaken;
3. the duration of the agreement;
4. the capital contributions—sources, amounts, formulas, etc.;
5. the formulas for dividing profit and loss;
6. the time of duty for partnership members;
7. salaries and drawing rights;
8. any restrictions;
9. rights of withdrawal;
10. insurance requirements and provisions in the event of death of a partner.

Consider also how to handle currency fluctuations, visa issues, or differing interpretations of copyright law. Decide your preferred legal system for handling a dispute if it reaches the point of a lawsuit. (You may or may not have a choice).

In developing a contractual agreement, consider the tax consequences. Often the type and amount of taxes to be paid will depend upon the legal structure of the entity engaged in the co-production—a proprietary corporation, a nonprofit corporation or trust, a partnership, or unincorporated individuals. The sources of income, the separation between operating and capital funds, and the address for the business are all factors that affect the taxes to be paid. Sometimes international ventures can be taxed twice—once by each country. The types of taxes—income, sales, or value

added (VAT) will vary from political jurisdiction to political jurisdiction. Each co-production project will require different answers to these questions. Just do the homework. Talk with a knowledgeable accountant and lawyer before the contract is finalized.

Similarly, you must consider insurance contracts for your production. Figure 2 illustrates some of the important coverage items to be considered.

You've already read an example of how a contract can influence the way in which a program is produced—the case of ABC sports and the 1991 Pan American Games. Another major corporation—the American Public Broadcasting System (PBS) operating through WGBH Boston works with its partners in "Nova" co-production contracts and in distribution contracts.

"Nova"'s requirement is to provide PBS stations with PBS distribution rights—That is, the right to air the program for 4 plays in 3 years. Each play comes with a repeat during the same 7 days. So, comments Acquisitions Director Alain Jehlan, "if we buy a film from abroad, we buy just those rights. Usually we also buy North American audiovisual rights because we have a distributor which sells and rents 'Nova' programs for schools, colleges, libraries, museums. It's for nontheatrical rights—you don't pay to get in. Museums are a gray area—you pay to get into the museum but not to get into the exhibit. Nontheatrical events are mostly in schools and libraries. Occasionally we skip the audiovisual rights. The criteria for deciding is usually money. We don't get foreign rights, because the producers are selling their film to other people. If this is a co-production, we also need the right to modify the film. It's called *versioning*. Sometimes it's a problem with someone we don't know because we often want to make major changes. A producer usually doesn't want his or her film changed by us."[27]

POLITICS

Ideology

The established political policy is the determining factor in deciding what is or is not possible in co-production. For those whose total experience is North American industrialized democracy, it's easy to overlook this factor for two reasons: (1) the constitutionally guaranteed and practiced freedoms make it possible to embark upon most projects, hassled perhaps by specific regulations and bureaucracy, but not prohibited, and (2) North America, specifically the United States, has been such a dominant force in communications technology and programming that, for Americans, anything has seemed possible.

However, never underestimate the importance of politics. The ABC experience trying to cover the Pan American Games in a country officially considered a political enemy of the United States is one illustration.

The EBU experience trying to secure news from the former communist bloc countries also illustrates how ideology can encourage or discourage cooperation. The EBU was seeking information on a trial in a political opposition case, and Pierre Brunel-Lantenac sent a telex to Prague asking for any news coverage of this trial. After two days' wait (because in those days Prague had to ask permission of Moscow), the answer came—we have "no item available on these so-called

PRODUCTION INSURANCE COVERAGE AREAS

Insurance brokers to the entertainment industry, present a brief description of the various types of insurance coverages available to the motion picture and television production company. These descriptions are general in nature and are not a complete explanation of the policy terms.

CAST INSURANCE

Reimburses the production company for any extra expense necessary to complete principal photography of an insured production due to the death, injury, or sickness of any insured performer or director. Insured performers (or director) must take a physical examination prior to being covered by this insurance. Physical examination cost to be paid by production company. Coverage begins two weeks prior to the beginning of principal photography.

NEGATIVE FILM AND VIDEOTAPE

Covers against all risks of direct physical loss, damage, or destruction of raw film or tape stock, exposed film (developed or undeveloped), recorded videotape, sound tracks and tapes, up to the amount of insured production cost.

COVERAGE DOES NOT INCLUDE loss caused by—fogging; faulty camera or sound equipment; faulty developing, editing, processing, or manipulation by the cameraman; exposure to light, dampness or temperature changes; or errors in judgment in exposure, lighting, or sound recording, or from the use incorrect type of raw film stock or tape.

FAULTY STOCK, CAMERA, AND PROCESSING

Covers loss, damage, or destruction of raw film or tape stock, exposed film (developed or undeveloped), recorded videotape, sound tracks and tapes caused by or resulting from fogging or the use of faulty materials (including cameras and videotape recorders); faulty sound equipment; faulty developing; faulty editing or faulty processing; and accidental erasure of videotape recordings.

COVERAGE DOES NOT INCLUDE loss caused by—errors of judgment in exposure, lighting, or sound recording, from the use of incorrect type of raw stock, or faulty manipulation by the cameraman.

This coverage can only be purchased with Negative Film and Videotape coverage.

PROPS, SETS, AND WARDROBE

Provides coverage on props, sets, scenery, costumes, wardrobe, and similar theatrical property against all risks or direct physical loss, damage, or destruction, during the production.

EXTRA EXPENSE

Reimburses the production company for any extra expense necessary to complete principal photography of an insured production due to the damage or destruction or property or facilities (props, sets, or equipment) used in connection with the production.

MISCELLANEOUS EQUIPMENT

Covers against all risks of direct physical loss, damage, or destruction to cameras, camera equipment, sound, lighting, and grip equipment, owned by or rented to the production company. Coverage can be extended to cover mobile equipment vans, studio location units, or similar units upon payment of an additional premium.

PROPERTY DAMAGE LIABILITY

Pays for damage or destruction of property of others (including loss of use of the property) while the property is in the care, custody, or control or the production company and is used or to be used in an insured production.

COVERAGE DOES NOT APPLY TO—Liability for destruction of property caused by operation of any motor vehicle, aircraft, or watercraft, including damage to the fore-

(continued)

▶ *Figure 2   Motion Picture and Television Insurance Coverages List. (Source: Truman Van Dyke Company, 6290 Sunset Boulevard, Suite 1900, Hollywood, CA 90023, tel.: 213-462-3300. Many other companies also provide such insurance.)*

going; Liability for damage to any property rented or leased that may be covered under Props, Sets or Wardrobe, or Miscellaneous Equipment insurance (EXCEPT, that loss of use of any such equipment is covered).

THIS INSURANCE IS NOT COVERED under a Comprehensive Liability Policy. Property Damage coverage written as part of a Comprehensive Liability Policy excludes damage to any property in the production company's care, custody, or control.

ERRORS AND OMISSIONS

Covers legal liability and defense for the production company against lawsuits alleging unauthorized use of titles, format, ideas, characters, plots, plagiarism, unfair competition, or breach of contract. Also protects for alleged libel, slander, defamation of character, or invasion of privacy. This coverage will usually be required by a distributor prior to release of any theatrical or television production.

WORKER'S COMPENSATION

This coverage is required to be carried by state law and applies to all temporary or permanent cast or production crew members. Coverage provides medical, disability, or death benefits to any cast or crew member who becomes injured in the course of their employment. Coverage applies on a 24 hour per day basis whenever employees are on location away from home.

Individuals who call themselves "Independent Contractors" will usually be held to be employees as far as Worker's Compensation is concerned, and failure to carry this insurance can result in having to pay any benefits required under the law plus penalty awards.

COMPREHENSIVE LIABILITY

Protects the production company against claims for Bodily Injury or Property Damage Liability arising out of filming the picture. Coverage includes use of all non-owned vehicles (both on and off camera), including physical damage to such vehicles. This coverage will be required prior to filming on any city or state roadways, or any location sites requiring filming permits.

COVERAGE DOES NOT APPLY TO use of any aircraft or watercraft and which must be separately insured before any coverage will apply.

GUILD/UNION FLIGHT ACCIDENT

Provides motion picture/television (IATSE/NABET/SAG/DGA) guild or union contract requirements for aircraft accidental death insurance to all production company cast or crew members. Coverage is blanket and the limits of liability meet all signatory requirements.

COMPLETION GUARANTY BOND

Completion Guaranty Bonds are available for feature motion picture productions that meet certain minimum budget requirements. Completion guaranty will provide completion funds for up to 100% of total picture budget.

These brief descriptions provide a simplified explanation of the various types of insurance protection available to motion picture or television production companies. Most of these coverages will have deductibles of varying amounts depending upon the limits of insurance coverage required. Premiums for theatrical features are based upon the size of the picture budget and will vary between 3 and 4% of the total budget, depending upon location site, length of shooting time, and any special hazards or stunts.

Commercial and documentary production companies can obtain annual Producers Insurance Policies (PIP policies) incorporating various combinations of film insurance coverages.

▶ *Figure 2*   (*continued*)

defectors."[28] Now, with political events at the end of the 1980s and the beginning of the 1990s, the situation has changed again. This particular type of repression is gone from both Czechoslovakia and the Soviet Union. The OIRT, from whom the EBU sought the news, no longer exists. With changes in politics, institutions also change. According to Lantenac, politics and institutions change, but attitudes may not be moved so easily. "People who have been told to function one way all their lives may not instantly know how to function a different way."[29]

Dr. Milan Smid, Professor of Electronic Media in the Faculty of Social Sciences at Charles University in Prague, identified another way in which politics affected co-production. "Before the revolution we did co-production because we had ideas and others had the money. But at that time, the ideas must be politically acceptable—so, we developed a tradition in producing fairy tales and lots of children's programming."[30]

Smid also notes that "before the revolution there was also much collaboration among countries within the eastern bloc. There was little possibility for collaboration with other countries. Now, there are many new projects. The ideological barriers are gone. We can work with any country. And because the ideological barriers are gone, the economic prohibitions are also gone. We're seeing expansion of private companies alongside the traditional public broadcaster."[31]

A curious variation on the effect of politics on international co-production—or at least collaboration—is the export of the fight between blacks in South Africa as portrayed in the world press in 1990 and 1991. Elsabe Wessels, TV Political Correspondent for the new independent television news launched in early 1992, notes, "this has been built up by the press as a big fight between ethnic groups. That it is not. But it comes across that way on the media. Enkatha, according to more than 35 surveys—many done by very conservative pollsters—has about 4% support among the South African population. The African National Congress (ANC), on the other hand, has on average 60% support or higher. This is not my bias. It's survey results. But note the political orientation of the two groups. Enkatha represents capitalism and free enterprise. ANC stands for a mixed economy with a socialist bias.

"These internationally shown news items are produced by the South African Broadcasting Corporation (SABC) in collaboration with those to whom it is exported. The production is all South African. CNN, one of the primary receivers of these programs, deals only with the finished product. CNN then uses it on its programs and makes it available to public and private broadcasters worldwide. Others are exported to the U.S. State Department for distribution throughout the world. So the SABC has a unit doing production for export. I was very surprised to learn this from the State Department and from CNN when I was in Washington and Atlanta. There's no knowledge of this in South Africa, yet material with a very strong political bias is exported, creating a different image of South Africa than that known by people living in the country."[32]

The message for the co-producer is that political bias shows up in many many places, and if one is concerned about the ethics of one's work, then it's always wise to examine the situation in which one works to see if the big picture and the small picture interpretations are the same.

Wessels highlights another form of political collaboration, co-financing production. "There's one other group. There's the independent group—Video News Service in Johannesburg. They are an independent unit that does feed outside the country. They do news and documentaries from a progressive point of view. It's financed mostly by foreign funding—NGOs, Sweden, Norway, and the Danish. The Nordic countries tend to fund most of the independent activity in South Africa.

"The Video News Service is known for their experience in covering the evolvement of the South African story. Whatever happened anywhere, they were there to film it. It's interesting because aside from the South African security police, who also filmed everything, Video News Service probably has the best documented library. SABC never covered anything—except for this outside unit. We never saw anything of black politics on SABC television. So whites in South Africa grew up thinking that there is only white politics—very nice, very reassuring. Just the life of the four million white people."

Wessels reminds us however, that "there's no such thing as an objective journalist. Every South African has a political bias. The issues are too crucial and people make choices." What's true in South Africa is true everywhere—all people make choices. Consequently, the person engaged in international co-production must be enough aware of the politics to know where the production rests on the spectrum of choices.

Government Advocacy

On a pragmatic level, politics and diplomacy can also help to grease the wheels of successful co-production projects. For example, independent filmmaker Herb Fuller talks about an American-Thai project. "Before you go abroad, know what you can about the embassies and consulates of your native country. You may need them to vouch for you with local customs officials—i.e., verify that this person *is* making a program and is not someone selling equipment on the black market. You may need them to explain laws or practices that are unfamiliar to you. In one situation, I wanted permission to visit a facility in a remote area of Thailand. I was told in Bangkok to get permission from local officials. I traveled some distance and got within a half mile of my destination and was told once there to get permission in Bangkok. Meanwhile in Bangkok, heads were rolling because of an unrelated accident where a civil servant had allowed a train to run into a vehicle owned by the royal family. The permission granting task of the bureaucracy was very low on the list of priorities carried by officials that week. In a monarchy, even a small offense can take on major proportions, if the offended party is royalty. A person traveling with tens of thousands of dollars worth of equipment may need a friend at her or his embassy."[33]

"You can't have a Ph.D. in the workings of every government you deal with, but a hint of knowledge doesn't hurt," says Fuller. "Capitalist countries, socialist countries, monarchies, democracies, and dictatorships differ greatly in mode of doing business. You can find out from a library how a given country is supposed to work, and you can know which agencies and people to contact if problems arise."[34]

ECONOMICS OF CO-PRODUCTION

Budget Realities

The costs of television production are high and going higher. Production costs include above line items such as on-air talent, producers, directors, and related production assistant personnel. Post-production costs of editing, multi-language versioning, voice-overs or subtitles, costs of maps or graphics, and standard conversions must all be included. Below-line costs are engineering staff, personnel for installing and maintaining facilities, facilities and equipment (cameras, tape decks, editing equipment, sound and lighting equipment, etc.), travel costs, satellite charges, business management overhead (including, administration, insurance, fringe benefits), and distribution costs. Then there's the cost of getting exposure—entering festivals, sending sample footage to stations. Expense, of course, is relative, based on the type and size of audience, how much money is available, and who controls that money. But whether one is an independent producer, a small company, an educational producer, a corporate producer, or a major broadcast producer, these costs are inescapable.

"Now, the challenge will be creativity—on a budget," is the *TV Guide* prediction about the 1990's.[35] According to Multimedia Chairman Walter Bartlett, "We have been in a media recession since the last quarter of 1989."[36] Co-production is frequently cited as one tool used to minimize the budget stretch.

"For public television, co-production is the nature of the beast," according to Suzanne Weil, senior vice president for programming for the U.S. Public Broadcasting Service. "At least three-quarters of the programs that make up the PBS schedule have more than one party involved."[37] Blaine Baggett, Executive Producer for national public affairs, from member station KCET TV, Los Angeles, states that foreign companies are just as much in need of partners for production. The money is shrinking everywhere—not just in America.[38]

Recognizing this financial difficulty, and acknowledging the fact that one-third of American public broadcasting prime time programming involves foreign interests, in early 1992 the Corporation for Public Broadcasting authorized $50,000 to develop a plan to create strategic alliances with international programming and funding sources. CPB seeks long-term program commitments with more direct contact with foreign programmers in order to ensure that programs are responsive to American audiences.[39]

In the field of documentary and educational program production, as Richard Sydenham of the United Nations states, "we're trying to get co-productions because we don't have much money, and we try to get corporate sponsorship." There are lots of possible contacts for collaboration—NGO's (nongovernmental organizations) around the world. For example, for our tape on literacy, six different NGOs provided footage of programs in the field to make a more rounded program. In that case, they had the footage and that saved the U.N. money.

"The main budget issue is what does funder want in exchange. Every time someone puts money in you lose some control."[40]

For the documentary and educational program producer in the United States,

commercial broadcasting finances all originate with the corporate sponsor. Most documentaries and educational programs would not be handled by these financiers because such programs are not productions for mass audiences. Documentaries and educational programs never will have money. Producers try to get what they can from sale to a cable network. PBS, Discovery, and the Arts & Entertainment (A&E) channels do take such programs, but what they pay may not cover the production costs. Often the stations themselves are trying to cut costs—first, to buy off the shelf, second, to put in completion money to finish or package film, and only third, to put money up front to make a production. If someone has a dynamite track record, they might buy in at the beginning.

The last few years of the 1980s saw American commercial television programs purchased at an ever increasing rate (and price) in Europe. It was easy programming for the host of new television stations. Italian entrepreneur Silvio Berlusconi would never have paid $500 for a half hour of "Death Valley Days" in the late 1970s. But in the late 1980s, he paid $70,000 per episode for the Italian rights to "Dynasty." In 1989, Hollywood made $800 million a year on sales to Europe.[41] Figure 3 shows the cost of syndicated programming in various countries.

In 1991, William Hearst, President of Hearst Entertainment, stated that 75% of the company's post-network revenue comes from abroad.[42] Meanwhile, in Europe, the 1992 European Economic Community directive, even if not enforced, has stimulated a European chauvinism, at a time when there's a considerable increase in the number of television channels to be programmed. The result will be a healthier mix of programming for Europe—with a lot of help from co-production. With new co-productions initiated abroad, and new technologies making it possible for a proliferation of stations in the United States, John Eger, President of Worldwide Media, noted that a reverse flow of programming may occur, that is, programs coming from Europe and other foreign countries to the United States to fill programming slots on cable channels.

The price of U.S. programming and the cost of producing entertainment programs has been a motivating factor for co-production. Three examples illustrate some of the new co-production activity that is appearing:

1. The German pay film channel Premiere was launched in spring 1991, a joint venture between Canal Plus, the first subscription channel in France, and the Kirch Group of France.
2. Beyond International of Australia, together with BBC, Spain's TVE, Sweden's SVT, France's Gideon, and RAI of Italy, produced a 10-part series, "Extra," on changes in Europe. They also involved Poltel of Poland and MTV of Hungary.[43]
3. In December 1991 the NHK Network in Japan together with its American co-producer ABC aired "Pearl Harbor: Two Hours That Changes The World." This 50th anniversary of Pearl Harbor show interviewed both Japanese and American survivors and was followed by a "town metting" in which ABC's Ted Koppel held a debate between an American audience and Koppel's Japanese guests on current Japanese-American attitudes and relationships.[44]

Cost of Syndicated Programming

COUNTRY	Half Hour Episode	Feature Film	TV System	Language
Algeria	$ 90- 100	$ no sales	PAL	Arabic- French
Argentina	1,000- 1,500	3,000- 6,000	PAL	Spanish
Australia	NA- NA	75,000- 500,000	PAL	English
Austria	900- 1,400	2,700- 5,000	PAL	German
Belgium	1,250- 1,750	5,000- 21,000	PAL	Dutch-German-French
Bermuda	30- 40	90- 150	NTSC	English
Brazil	4,000- 6,000	15,000- 30,000	PAL	Portuguese
Bulgaria	200- 250	500- 1,000	SECAM	Bulgarian
Canada	6,000- 20,000	up to 300,000	NTSC	English-French
Chile	220- 375	6,000- 10,000	NTSC	Spanish
China, P.R.	350-1500		PAL	Mandarian
Colombia	800- 1,500	2,000- 5,000	NTSC	Spanish
Costa Rica	180- 210	1,200- 1,750	NTSC	Spanish
Cyprus	30- 75	100- 275	PAL	Greek-Turkish-English
Czechoslovakia	400- 600	2,000- 3,000	SECAM	Czechish
Denmark	700- 900	3,500- 4,000	PAL	Denish
Dominican Republic	100- 150	225- 300	NTSC	Spanish
East Germany	750- 1,500	6,000- 10,000	PAL	German
Ecuador	200- 300	1000- 6,000	NTSC	Spanish
Egypt	400- 600	1,750- 2,500	SECAM	Arabic
El Salvador	75- 90	550- 625	NTSC	Spanish
Finland	900- 1,000	3,500- 4,000	PAL	Finish
France	8,500- 10,000	30,000- 40,000	SECAM	French
Gibraltar	40- 94	125- 300	PAL	English
Greece	700- 750	3,000- 3,750	SECAM	Greek
Guatemala	100- 125	600- 1,200	NTSC	Spanish
Haiti	50- 75	100- 200	SECAM	French--Creole
Honduras	85- 90	300- 400	NTSC	Spanish
Hong Kong	600- 850	6,500- 10,000	PAL	Chinese
Hungary	200- 300	1,300- 1,800	SECAM	Hungarian
India	500- 600	12,000- 20,000	PAL	Hindi-English
Iran	500- 750	3,000- 4,000	SECAM/V	Kurdish-Arabic
Iraq	350- 500	1,200- 2,000	SECAM/V	Arabic-Kurdish
Ireland	300- 350	1,200- 1,400	PAL	English
Israel	400- 500	1,200- 4,000	SECAM/V	Hebrew-Arabic-Eng.
Italy	6,000- 48,000	20,000- 75,000	PAL	Italian
Jamaica	80- 95	300- 400	NTSC	English
Japan	6,000- 7,000	60,000- 200,000	NTSC	Japanese
Kenya	45- 60	110- 150	PAL	Swahili-Bantu-English
Kuwait	450- 500	1,750- 2,000	SECAM/V	Arabic-English
Lebanon	175- 200	800- 900	SECAM/V	Arabic-French-Eng.
Luxembourg	1,200- 1,500	20,000- 75,000	PAL	Letzeburgesch-French
Malaysia	400- 850	1,500- 3,400	PAL	Malay-Chinese
Malta	45- 50	150- 250	PAL	Maltese-English
Mexico	1,000- 2,000	10,000- 50,000	NTSC	Spanish
Monaco	400- 450	1,200- 1,700	SECAM	French
Netherlands	2,000- 2,250	7,500- 8,500	PAL	Dutch
New Zealand	625- 700	1,800- 3,000	PAL	English-Maori
Nicaragua	75- 85	300- 500	NTSC	Spanish
Nigeria	1,000- 1,500	5,000- 6,000	PAL	English-Native Tongues
Norway	900- 1,000	3,500- 4,000	PAL	Norwegian
Panama	200- 215	800- 3,000	NTSC	Spanish
Peru	250- 300	1,800- 2,000	NTSC	Spanish
Philippines	250- 600	3,000- 12,000	NTSC	Philipino-English-
Poland	150- 375	1,000- 1,600	SECAM	Polish
Portugal	215- 500	1,200- 2,000	PAL	Portuguese
Puerto Rico	1,100- 1,250	6,000- 20,100	NTSC	Spanish
Rumania	200- 450	1,000- 1,800	SECAM	Rumanian
Saudi Arabia	650- 800	3,000- 3,200	SECAM/V	Arabic
Singapore	300- 500	1,000- 1,700	PAL	Malay-Chinese
South Africa	1,250- 1,800	350- 425	PAL	English-Afrikaans-
South Korea	750- 1,000	up to 25,000	NTSC	Korean
Spain	1,500- 2,500	7,800- 18,000	PAL	Spanish
Sweden	2,100- 2,500	10,000- 40,000	PAL	Swedish
Switzerland	1,500- 2,000	4,000- 9,000	PAL	German-French-Italian
Syria	70- 275	150- 1,250	SECAM	Arabic
Taiwan	300- 400	4,000- 20,000	NTSC	Chinese-Cantonese
Thailand	500- 750	2,400- 3,000	PAL	Thai-Siamese-Chinese
Trinidad, Tobago	130- 140	500- 560	NTSC	English-Hindi
United Kingdom	12,000- 14,000	60,000- 3MIL	PAL	English
Uruguay	800- 1,000	2,500- 5,000	NTSC	Spanish
USSR	120-300	6,000- 8,000	SECAM	Russian
Venezuela	800- 1,000	2,500- 5,000	NTSC	Spanish
West Germany	8,500- 18,000	50,000- 59,000	PAL	German
Yugoslavia	175- 500	1,100- 2,000	PAL	Serbo-Slovene

▶ *Figure 3* *Global Prices for U.S. Television Films. (Source: "Global Prices for U.S. Films,"* Television International, *Vol. 32, No. 5 [Fall/Spring 1989–1990]. Television International, P.O. Box 2430, Hollywood, CA 90028, fax: 818-795-8436.)*

Funding Strategies

How do producers find financing? This, of course, varies, depending upon who owns the production: a government station or agency, an independent public broadcasting system, a private commercial station, a small private company, a nonprofit charitable institution, or an individual. Finding funds for a co-production will depend in part on how the organization embarking on the co-production is structured, in part on who is approached with a request, in part on timing, and in large part on the imagination and the stamina of the person seeking the funds. A blend of funding is likely: government money, investors, individual support, grants, presales to a station, bartering, and other forms of linking resources in the process of collaborating.

Government funds   Government grants have been sources of financing for producers for decades. The resources available in the United States at all three levels of government—federal, state, and local—are much less than they were in the 1960s and 1970s. However, in the 1990s there is still money available. See the references identified in Chapter 6. You'll want to learn more about the National Endowment for the Arts (NEA), the National Endowment for the Humanitites (NEH), the Public Broadcasting System (PBS), and the Corporation for Public Broadcasting (CPB), as well as a host of other agencies. Some agencies will contract for tapes and film because they see it in their self-interest to have such a product to show their constituencies, even through their primary mission may be housing or transportation or defense, not video production.

In many countries of the world, television is principally government financed through fees on TV receivers. Aside from regular fee-financed local production in a given country, some types of co-production are fee financed, for example, the news productions of the EBU discussed in Chapter 2. Pierre Brunel-Lantenac of the EBU states, "I'm proud of EBU because it is the only organization I know where we have established the principle of equality of all our members. The EBU is financed by member station fees. The fees take into account the financial possibilities of all our countries. Tunisia will pay peanuts. Paris and Rome pay a lot because they have the capacity to pay. This is I think important to keep up the free flow of information."[45]

Major government funding becomes available with major government policy shifts. The European Economic Community provides a major focal point for new production resources in the 1990s. The creative producer will realize that policy shifts affect private funding sources as well as government resources. This is because the private sector wants to take advantage of (or not be hurt by) new market shifts.

Vade Mecum is a report published periodically by the European Community for the purpose of providing film and television professionals with information about the developments and changes in the EC Media program.[46] The EC Media Progam Management have created a number of programs. Examples are listed in the following paragraphs.

The MEDIA (*M*easures to *E*ncourage the *D*evelopment of the *I*ndustry of *A*udiovisual Production) program of the European Community promises many new avenues for producers. Media Venture has been established, a venture capital fund

created to finance the production and distribution of high budget commercial films and television series.[47]

The European Film Distribution Office (EFDO) was created to sponsor European films, especially low-budget films. To qualify for EFDO aid, co-productions must have originated in an EC country, Switzerland, or Austria or have majority participation by production firms based in these countries.

Espace Video Europeen (EVE) is the organization created to support film culture in Europe by encouraging effective publication and distribution of a European film or video. Among other things, EVE provides loans and grants to companies that are producers or owners of video publication rights. To be eligible, publishers or distributors of international co-production must have EC co-production partners who have participated to the amount of at least 51% of the total production cost.

Broadcasting Across the Barriers of European Language (BABEL) is the fund for multilingual audiovisual production. BABEL provides funds for dubbing and subtitling programs that have received a broadcast commitment from a television station.

A European organization called EURO-AIM was founded for audiovisual independent markets. Its purpose is to provide support for independent producers in marketing, promoting, and selling their productions. Primarily, EURO-AIM would like to bring more European independent productions to the attention of international buyers. Its first achievement was to bring 230 independent producers to the MIPCOM 1988 festival, where, with shared screening facilities and marketing experts, the producers were able to sell more than 400 hours of independent programming.[48]

SCRIPT is the European Script Fund to which writers can apply for funding to support the writing and development of scripts and to help artists prepare a product ready for the final stages of production. Eligible applicants come from the EC states, Switzerland, or Austria.

CARTOON (the European Association for Animation Films) is the organization that provides assistance in the development of animation techniques, preproduction help and help in networking among European animation studios. Eligible applicants are nationals of the EC member states who plan to do all their preproduction work in Europe.

MAP-TV (Memory, Archives, Programs) is an association of production and archive organizations. Its purpose is to foster co-production that can enhance the preservation of European identity.

European Audiovisual Entrepreneurs (EAVE) was created to innovate and improve systems of production and co-production in order to stimulate collaboration that favors the advancement of European audiovisual entrepreneurs. Its assistance comes mainly through bringing together appropriate groups in workshops.

Many individual countries support film and video through their Ministries of Culture (Spain) or Ministries of Tourism (Italy) or entities like the Danish Film Institute or the Dutch Film Production Board. Identify the appropriate agency in the country where your co-production will be based.

Outside the EC, however, it is difficult in the 1990s to find so elaborate a network of government financing. The EC motivation is to compete with the American

film and video industry. European member states are economically able to make such competition a realistic objective. The EC catalyst for action is the 1992 date for creation of a single European market.

No other section of the world benefits from the combination of incentive to excel, the economic viability to make objectives possible, and a real time deadline.

Japan has the economic viability to support such growth in the video industry. Japanese firms are beginning to take part in the co-productions. To date, however, the principal Japanese involvement has been private sector acquisition of properties and developing co-ventures in the business partnership sense (like the NNBC project discussed in Chapter 2).

The South East Asian Alliance (ASEAN) is increasingly developing as a parallel to the European Economic Community. A communications revolution is coming to this region of the world. The technology is arriving, and the political atmosphere is less restrictive. The purpose of ASEAN is to unite Pacific Basin neighbors—especially Japan, China, and Korea—to increase the region's importance in the global market. It may be after the start of the 21st century before government resources for television co-production are available, but it bears watching.

The former Eastern European bloc countries have a strong incentive for developing their film and television industries in the new climate free from political repression. Their governments do not have the money, however. Co-production possibilities remain the best option in that it is possible to combine the use of government facilities available for production with foreign supplied hard currency needed for other aspects of the project.

Access to government money depends in part on politics. If the government funds television and film production, it is more accessible if the party in power is friendly.

Private funding   For corporate funding, personal access to the owners always helps. Philanthropic funding is available through foundations and individual donors.

Individual purchases of shares or tickets or tapes seem insignificant to the producer who needs start-up capital. Just look at the profits, however, that come from such sales of a Hollywood film. Just as individual donations constitute the largest source of philanthropic giving, so the individual sale is, in the last analysis, the money maker in the private entrepreneurial sector. The only problem is start-up funding—to produce the product and market it.

Resource libraries exist and workshops are held on the topic of funding strategies. For lists of organizations that have such resources, see Chapter 6.

While analyzing the following ideas used to fund projects, don't forget that a successful production may combine as many different methods of fund-raising as are necessary to accomplish the task.

One producer got an investment bank line of credit for several hundred thousand dollars. She initiated a co-production involving both U.S. and U.K. professionals. Her plan was to use the pool of funds, committed actors, and a miniseries contract to show the production on a cable network. One appeal for the idea in Britain was the idea of showcasing British actors and production people to the

American audience. When she contacted funders, she had a distribution contract in hand. It was a good package and proved to be a success.

Another producer looked for tax incentives to entice potential funders. Some countries give tax incentives to those who will finance productions. One route to tax incentives in the United States is that friends and family can invest in your venture in return for some tax benefits as business expenses. Also, a person can give you a gift of up to $10,000 per year without tax consequences for either donor or receiver. Check carefully to be sure you and the person investing in your project understand the Internal Revenue Service tax code regulations before pursuing any actual transactions. If you carry this form of investment to the point of raising money through limited partnerships, where the donor does not have control of the project, or through some form or business corporation, be sure to consult an experienced entertainment business lawyer and a knowledgeable tax accountant before you finalize any agreements.

Private foundations, such as Guggenheim, Ford, and Rockefeller give grants to individuals for creative work. Many other foundations that might be interested in your project may be approached. Consult the Foundation Center Library and related funding directories (see references in Chapter 6). Watch the credits on independently produced films, PBS documentaries, and other programs appealing to your audience to identify potential funding sources.

Bartering   Different kinds of bartering exist. Many of the former Eastern Bloc countries are making bartering agreements because they have no convertible currency. For example, a Western television entity might provide Western television equipment in return for video or film footage. Or, a program viewing may be bartered for free advertising time.

Another type of bartering is the trades done as a form of program sponsorship. WDR Director of Production, Manfred Jenke, calls for guidelines for sponsors and for bartering. These frequently used approaches for financing productions may create the cash, but they also create some ethical problems. "We have self-imposed guidelines to prevent certain kinds of sponsoring or bartering that might result in conflict of interest, but the boundaries are fuzzy. For example, say a sponsor wants to finance a series on good cooking and is prepared to undertake such a co-production under the condition that the program features the sponsor's kitchen products. At WDR, that would not be allowed. It would be allowed if there is not direct advertising. The problem is where do the credits end and where does the advertising begin?[49] This temptation is a common one for those starved for production financing. If a hotel will sponsor a production in return for featuring the hotel in the film, what does one do? There must be a good reason in the story for including the credit from a given hotel—perhaps only that this hotel is near a cathedral featured in the film. The problem could also materialize if a car dealer is willing to finance a detective story as long as the detectives always drive the cars of the same manufacturer.

What's legitimate sponsoring? What's legitimate bartering? What's manipulating the audience?

Pay-as-you-go funding For the small independent producer, options are sometimes quite limited—until one has produced enough to have contacts and to have one's work recognized. Herb Fuller recounted, "my first international production I bankrolled myself. It was on steam locomotives in England. I co-produced it with an individual I met in England and used my own home movie equipment. There was no money for anything. I'll never forget it. There was no place to store equipment. It was a small town, and I couldn't even rent a car. So I went to the exhibition tent at the event where we filmed and rented the boot [trunk] of the car in exhibition in order to store my equipment so I could shoot. It's how you get started."[50]

Philosophy of Financing

Don't let yourself get mired in the quicksand of fund-raising procedure and technique without keeping your eye firmly fixed on the overall objective. Dighton Spooner from Granada Television in London remarks, "Budgets are statements of creative intent. Move backward from the creative to the budget. The goal is to create programs that might not have been produced otherwise—that have larger scope and vision."[51]

Notes

1. Sidney W. Head, World Broadcasting Systems: A Comparative Analysis (Belmont, California: Wadsworth, 1985), p. 158.
2. Ibid.
3. U.S. Copyright Office, Library of Congress, Washington, DC 20559, tel.: 202-287-9100. This office can send you information brochures and forms for filing for copyright. In a library with federal documents, one can read the law itself. Also see Alan Richardson and Thomas Schwartz, "What Media Managers Should Know about copyrights," *Educational and Industrial Television Journal*, EITV, (Broadband Information Services, Inc., 295 Madison Ave., New York, NY 10017, tel.: 212-685-5320), October 1982, p. 74f. Also see Ronald H. Gertz Esq., "What a Producer Needs to Know About Copyrights," International Tape Association (ITA) News Digest (ITA, 10 Columbus Circle, Suite 2270, New York, NY 10019, tel.: 212-956-7110), September-October 1982.
4. Personal interview with Lydia Stephans, Director, Programming, ABC Sports, 47 West 66th Street, New York, NY 10023, tel.: 212-456-3702, August 23, 1991.
5. Ibid.
6. Ibid.
7. Morris Crawford, *The Common Market for Telecommunications and Information Services,* (Cambridge, Harvard University Center, Mass.: for Information Policy Research, 1990), p. 1.
8. Fred H. Cate, "The European Broadcasting Directive" (Washington, D.C.: American Bar Association, Section of International Law and Practice, Communications Committee, Monograph Series 1990/1, April 1990).
9. Ibid. Also see minutes of Committee Session, 101st Congress, First Session, 50, 1989, Statement of Richard Frank.
10. Ibid, p. 8.
11. Ibid. pp. 8–9.

12. Ibid. p. 9
13. Personal interview with Dr. Manfred Jenke, Director of Broadcasting, Westdeutscher Rundfunk, Appellhofplatz 1, Postfach 10 19 50, 5000 Koln, Germany, fax: 49-221-220-3539, tel.: 49-221-220-4140, February 27, 1991. Also see Wachter interview.
14. Personal interview with Dighton E. Spooner, Jr., Executive Vice President, Films for Television, Grenada Television, 36 Golden Square, London W1R 4AH, England, fax: 213-282-8992, tel.: 213-282-8996, February 15, 1991.
15. Janet Watson, Editor, *Co-Production Europe* (IPPA, 50-51 Berwick St., London W1A-41D, tel.:44-71-439-7034, Fax: 44-71-494-2700, 1990), pp. 266–276.
16. Films Branch, Department of Trade and Industry, Kingsgate House, 66–74 Victoria Street, London SW1E 6SW, England, tel.: 44-071-215-2678.
17. Watson, pp. 257ff, pp. 287–288.
18. Head, p. 167.
19. Ibid., p. 168.
20. Ibid., p. 176ff.
21. "Reporting the Gulf War," a Communications Forum Panel sponsored by the MIT Center for Technology, Policy and Industrial Development, MIT, Cambridge, Mass., October 17, 1991.
22. Ibid.
23. Harry Mums, "Shooting Through the Iron Curtain," *Videography* (Videography, 2 Park Avenue, New York, NY, tel.: 212-213-3444), May 1990, p. 33.
24. Personal interview with Herb Fuller, independent filmmaker, 54 Preston Road, Somerville, MA 02143, August 13, 1991.
25. Ibid.
26. Sydenham interview and his pass-out used for workshop on international co-production.
27. Personal interview with Alain Jehlan, Director of Acquisitions, "Nova," WGBH, Boston, August 27, 1991.
28. Personal interview with Pierre Brunel-Lantenac, Director, News Operations, European Broadcasting Union, Ancienne Route 17a/Casa Postale 67, CH-1218 Grand Saconnex, Geneva, Switzerland, Fax: 022-798-5897, tel.: 022-717-2821, February 22, 1991.
29. Ibid.
30. Personal interview with Milan Smid, Ph.D., Assistant Professor, Electronic Media Department, Faculty of Arts and Sciences, Charles University, Praha 1, Smetanovo nabrezi 6, Czechoslovakia, May 10, 1991 at New Century Policies Journalists' Workshop, c/o Emerson College's Kasteel Well, Well, Limburg, The Netherlands.
31. Ibid.
32. Personal interview with Elsabe Wessels, M-NET TV Political Correspondent, Johannesburg, South Africa, October 8, 1991.
33. Personal interview with Herb Fuller, independent filmmaker, 54 Preston Road, Somerville, MA 02143, August 13, 1991.
34. Ibid.
35. Herma M. Rosenthal and Ileane Rudolph, "Some Bright Spots Glimmer Despite TV's Darkening Economic Picture," *TV Guide* (Radnor, PA: New America Publications, Inc., November 10-16, 1990), p. 49.
36. "1991: TV's Next Decade Is in with a Whimper," *Broadcasting,* Vol. 119, No. 19, November 5, 1990, p. 27.

37. Ibid.

38. Ibid.

39. "Washington Watch," *Broadcasting,* Vol. 121, No. 48, December 2, 1991, p. 54.

40. Personal interview with Richard Sydenham, Producer, Special Programs Section, Department of Information, United Nations, Room S-955, New York, NY 10017, Fax: 212-963-4556, tel.: 212-963-6944.

41. "Will European TV Quotas Ruin U.S. Programming," *Television International,* (Television International, P.O. Box 2430, Hollywood, CA 90028, Fax: 818-795-8436), Vol. 32, No.5, Fall/Spring 89–90.

42. "Prognosis for International TV," *Broadcasting,* Vol. 121, No. 13, September 23, 1991, p. 52.

43. "European Communiqué from the MIPCOM Front," *Broadcasting,* Vol. 119, No. 16, October 15, 1990, p. 32.

44. Jay Sharbutt, "ABC's 'Pearl Harbor' is a Standout," *The Boston Globe,* December 5, 1991, p. 58.

45. Lantenac interview.

46. "Vade Mecum: MEDIA '92," (Commission of the European Communities, Directorate of General Information, Communications and Culture, 200, Rue de la Loi, B-1049 Brussels, Belgium, tel.:02-235-11-11, fax: 02-236-42-77), Edition 5, October 1990.

47. Media Venture, 55 avenue Everard, 1190 Brussels, Belgium, tel.:32-2-345-7478.

48. "Vade Mecum: MEDIA '92," p. 112.

49. Jenke interview.

50. Fuller interview.

51. Spooner interview.

4

▼
▼
▼ **Production Process,**
▼ **Culture, and Technology**
▼

As the examples in Chapters 2 and 3 indicate, international co-production requires careful planning. Concurrent to developing the appropriate legal and contractual agreements, one must determine what's required to complete the production process, whether cultural and technological realities require special supplies or equipment, and what alternative plans must be prepared.

INTERNATIONAL CO-PRODUCTION PROCESS

Acquiring Services

Assembling the right team of people for your production takes on new dimensions when working in an international context. Obviously, one reason for engaging in co-production is to team up with other people to save money. The question is how best to accomplish the objective.

Evaluate the trade-offs in using crews based at the location for the shoot versus paying travel, and in renting equipment abroad versus shipping it. What are the advantages of combining crew and equipment resources—some of yours and some of your co-producer's—or contracting with a foreign production house? Eric Johnston, President of Johnston and Associates, a Boston-based production house, notes, "These arrangements generally come from personal referrals. I've had people call me from Los Angeles looking for a crew in Boston. They called because they had gotten my name from colleagues in New York. People do the obvious: they hire those who they think will be the most reliable—that is, those they have worked with before or those recommended by someone they trust. Only when this approach doesn't work do they find a name in a directory. Then, check carefully. Who will be assigned to the actual job? What is that person's background and experience? Has he or she done similar work to the kind that you want? For whom? Do these potential contractors provide their own equipment? If so, is it adequate? If not, what are your rental options? Can the persons or firms with whom you contract provide all of what you need, or must you supplement either the human resources or the equipment? How do they handle breakdowns and related emergency situations?

"A few years ago I was working on a shoot for a Boston firm, Active Video. We were on location in New Jersey. The client was flying in from Australia and had very little time. The shot was to be done in PAL format, not common equipment in the

U.S. We rented the equipment from a New York firm. Fortunately, the company was reliable because the deck malfunctioned. We made one telephone call, and a replacement deck was delivered to us before we reached our next location. That kind of reliability is critical."[1]

Another producer, Richard Sydenham, describes his preferred mode of operation when producing U.N. documentaries. "We have a full in-house production capability. But the work I do is often with outside companies. For example, if we can hook up with an outside company that already has a good track record in the subject matter, they may be able to contribute stock footage to increase the value of our production and save us money.

"When we look for private contractors, we examine the contacts of the person, the quality of their work—what they can bring to help our program that someone else would not be able to offer. It's not hard to hire a crew. It is hard to get someone who can contribute to the product. For example, with our peacekeeping educational video, we worked with an independent producer who was in the process of shooting a PBS special on the role of U.N. peacekeeping forces around the world. We thought that would be an ideal linkage. They contributed footage and their expertise. They'd already done a year or eighteen months of research and were well acquainted with the subject matter. So with our small budget we put together a very good program. In fact it was nominated for an award at the International Educational TV Festival.

"Another example of developing a production team for a U.N. project was when the U.N. contributed an on-camera spokesperson, an Irish Army Lieutenant Colonel who works in the U.N. building in New York, and the in-house U.N. production crews could shoot his on-camera pieces right at the U.N. headquarters."[2]

Sydenham prefers to take a New York–based crew with him to do shoots abroad. He says, "As a producer I want to work with someone whose work I'm familiar with. I want to have some assurance that the product will be quality. A demonstration reel from some company that I could hire on site might be fabricated and may not be an honest representation of the person's skills. I like to travel with as few unknown variables as possible." There are many variables to be dealt with in international production: logistics, travel, currencies, getting money out of the bank. If you take a cameraman whom you know, it might minimize the surprises. The trade-off in taking a crew or hiring one abroad is one of travel cost. Costs abroad may not be cheaper. They certainly are not cheaper if you have problems created because those you hired didn't deliver the product as you wanted it.

"Another factor in hiring crews and equipment abroad is the equipment format," says Sydenham. "But I wanted to use betacam equipment and I wanted NTSC format and most of the world uses PAL format. That's another decision. You could shoot PAL, which is inherently a better system, but then you have to do a conversion. PAL is a 625-line system, inherently better, but you lose so much in the conversion system. If you have to convert, it's better from PAL to NTSC than the other way around, to end up with the best possible product."[3]

Crew and Equipment Abroad

If you decide to find crew and equipment outside the United States, the skills of the people and the quality of the equipment to some extent depend on the country in

which you look. The industrialized democracies of Western Europe and the Pacific Basin have highly skilled people available and high quality equipment. You may have to do little more than check references before you make individual judgments. But Meg Gottemoeller, President of World Information Corporation, notes, "In some of the developing countries lack of training and inadequate facilities have resulted in lack of skilled professionals. For example, in Mexico there's virtually no training opportunities for would-be producers. The One World Trust has tried to help raise the standards of production. Countries like Hong Kong and India with huge film industries have well trained crews. Then again, countries like Czechoslovakia have a healthy tradition in producing high quality films but much less experience in video translation."[4]

If you want to hire a production company, remember that they operate differently in different parts of the world. Tony Goodman, Deputy Director of the International Visual Communications Association (IVCA) comments on the differences between his native London and working with production companies on the European continent. "European production companies work very differently from the corporate market in the U.K. Here in the U.K. it's like shoe buying. You go to the shop, see lots of shoes, try some, buy one. The shop pays up front for its premises and stock. You don't want to know about their cash flow—just their shoes. So here if a company wants to hire a production firm to produce a training video or to provide some service, that's a pair of shoes. The company goes to a number of production companies and asks what they can do. The competing production companies pitch [bid] for a job. They get no money for this. It's expensive. Production companies can put up lots of money and get nothing back. The advertising companies don't work that way. They have a client and they do the whole range of ads targeted toward a corporate brief stating where the company wants its image, its logo, its future use, its culture, etc. The corporations and producers who want the services of a video production house don't think that way yet.

"On the mainland, production houses already work like advertising agencies. You contract with the production house—perhaps for three years, and they satisfy your needs during that period. In some respects, you can make film the same way the world over, but if you're hiring a production house for certain kinds of services, the client relationship can differ greatly depending upon the firm's location."[5]

One mode of operation for an independent producer whose workplace is the globe is described below. "I did some editing work for an individual with a unique approach to his job," comments Eric Johnston. "He traveled the world to major sporting events. There he hired local crews to interview athletes for his marketplace. He made a deal with Transworld Sports and had the one-inch finished tape of major events flown by Concord into New York City. We met at a studio and shot a segment in the control room. Then we edited the program, adding his introduction, his interviews, and a narration in Spanish. The program was immediately uplinked and distributed throughout South America."[6]

If you are an independent producer without much budget and without a lot of institutional support, an international co-production may require other innovative ways of finding foreign resources. Independent filmmaker Herb Fuller suggests, "Look up American networks and find out who their stringers are in the location

near where you'll be. This is a source for expanding your crews. It's also a source for an inventory of NTSC compatible equipment—probably not used between news stories—possibly available for rental."[7]

Two agencies that provide production crews around the world are Worldwide Television News Corporation (WTN) and Visnews, LTD. Both are based in London. In difficult financial times the major television networks have reduced their foreign news bureaus. WTM and Visnews are filling the gap. The companies have existed since the 1950s, but their role providing critical coverage for major networks is recent.

WTN is now 80% owned by the U.S. network ABC. The balance of the company is owned by Channel Nine Australia and Britain's Independent Television News. Visnews is 51% owned by Reuters, the British news agency, with the remainder owned by America's NBC and the BBC. CBS contracts with Visnews. WTN and Visnews hire local workers and freelancers for their crews throughout the world. It's cheaper than hiring American veteran correpondents.[8]

Equipment Packing

Perhaps you decide to take your own equipment with you. If your co-production involves a major network, you'll not have to think about the details—simply play your assigned role as part of the team of people dealing with the peculiarities of a given situation. The ABC/TNT story of carrying equipment to Cuba is probably one of the more extreme cases of large-scale equipment moving logistics.

If you are an independent producer or part of a small company, the problems may be quite different. How much will they allow you to take on the plane rather than sending it as baggage? Will it get broken? If your luggage is over weight and you have more than two pieces, will you have to pay for excess baggage? Rules on the amount and cost may be different when you leave a country than they were when you entered the country. If you have to pay excess, plan ahead to have the right currency (or travelers checks if you are not certain that they take credit cards—some developing countries don't).

Do you have a battery charger and enough batteries to do the necessary work between charging? Do you have electrical power converters? Do you have enough tape stock? Do you have lights, microphones with enough cable? Without the equipment, you can't do your job. Figure 4 is an equipment list prepared by Richard Sydenham.[9]

"X rays and magnets are another thing you want to be aware of when transporting your equipment," notes independent filmmaker Herb Fuller. "There's a flux in inspection technology; they'll usually tell you not to worry. But I assume all is damaging to magnetic material. I use lead shields. I think this is important for checked luggage too. There's a claim that some checked luggage is x-rayed with more virulent x ray. It's best to be cautious; your whole project could be ruined otherwise. There are lead shield pouch bags in camera stores."[10]

Communicating with the security officials about their x-ray machines can pose a challenge when they don't speak English and you don't speak their language. Do you let your materials be ruined? Do you, in desperation, slip them some money? What if you're caught? Do you call for help—somewhere? Do you present them a note in their language explaining the situation? Plan ahead.

EQUIPMENT LIST		
Item	Brand/Model	Serial No.
Camera case		
Camera	Ampex CVR200	XXXX
Lens	Fuji A 14x8.5 BERM	XXXX
Camera mic		
Battery (2)	NP1A	
Filters	Clear, ND 6	
Rain cover		
Videotape		
Sound case		
Audio mixer	Shure FP-31	
Recorder	Sony WM-D6C	XXXX
Mic, shotgun	Sennheiser MKH-416	XXXX
Mic pre-amp	PSC MP-48	XXXX
Mic, lav.	Sony ECM-44B	XXXX
Mic, dynamic	Shure SM 631	XXXX
Headset	Sony NRD-V4	
Zepplin	Rycote	
Fishpole	LTM 613-90	
Mic cables, (4)		
Battery (2)	NP1A	
Batt. charger	Sony BC-1WA	XXXX
Audio tape, video tape		
MISC: audio adaptor kit, white card, assorted batteries		
Tripod case		
Tripod/head		
Spreader		
Light case		
Spotlights (2)		
Floodlight		
Camera light/cable		
Sun gun		
Battery belt/cable		
Light stands (3)		
AC cables (3)		
AC cables (2)		
AC splitter box		
Folding reflector/bracket		
110/220 power adaptors (4)		
Plug adaptor kits (2)		
MISC: gels, diffusion screen, clamps, spare bulbs		
General case		
Monitor	SONY PVM-8020	XXXX
Batteries (4)	NP1A	
Batt. charger	SONY BC-1WA	XXXX
AC cables (3)		
MISC: gaffers tape, camera tape, tool kit, fuses/spare parts		
Stock case		
Videotape (40)		

▶ *Figure 4   Sample Production Equipment List.*

Ground Transportation on Site

Finding a way to get your crew and equipment to the shoot can prove challenging in developing countries. While you may, or may not, be able to plan ahead, thinking about the logistics can help you plan for contingencies.

Herb Fuller provides some examples. "The large number of lockable vehicles that Americans consider a birthright are scarce in many developing countries. In Thailand, the largest closable lockable vehicle is a minivan. That was too small for us. But it was either that or a flatbed truck with a tarp—not secure, and way too big. In Thailand we needed a boat to ferry equipment. We found one. We carefully balanced our equipment to prevent it from falling overboard on this precarious vehicle. All of a sudden, other people jumped on. That's the way it works. Whoever wants to go, goes. Everyone just stands up. The boat had become a bathtub going over a malaria-filled body of water with our equipment just inches from the water. We shifted our priorities from watching the balance of the equipment to watching the others on board in hopes that they didn't make any sudden moves that might wash away our whole project.

"We had another transportation problem in Thailand. We needed aerial shots for our client. But in Thailand civilians can't own helicopters, so to do helicopter shots you must make deals with the military. Much time was lost because the military was offering not only deals for helicopters, but also officers' quarters for crew while they scuttled the official permissions we needed to film what we needed. The project was completed successfully; not easily.

"In Madeira, the Portuguese island off the west coast of Africa, we had other transportation challenges. Our client was an American travel video company working in collaboration with the Ministry of Tourism in Madeira. It had been arranged that we would shoot features of certain places and people where funding had been provided to help sponsor the event. In some cases hotels gave food and lodging in exchange for an 'infomercial' production where they were a setting. The Embroidery Institute paid something and we filmed the embroidery process and the certification process. Business persons representing the wicker trade paid and we filmed their facility. Doing our own driving of equipment was out of the question. We did all our equipment transporting in taxis—we wore out our welcome with some of the drivers. No amount of tip would overcome their not wanting to deal with the amount of stuff we had. And then, even if the driver was interested in transporting us, there might be a question of trunk space. Trunks were often full of the driver's possessions—a radio, a bucket, detergent, rags, tools. In some cases they might be living out of the trunk. No doubt, it was a memorable experience."[11]

Weather Patterns

Don't forget to think about which weather patterns will work for you. Do you want to shoot during monsoon season or "the cap of clouds"? One co-production got great financial help—free accommodations and food for the crew. But it was during the one month that no one came to this hotel because the weather was so terrible—not the best setting for filming a travel promotion.

CULTURE

Numerous cultural differences arise during international production and co-production. CNN International is seen in somewhere from 125 to 160 countries, reaching all the world's cultures, religions, value systems, and political systems. "It's not easy to accommodate cultural, political, and ethnic concerns which are mutually contradictory," comments CNN International Vice President Peter Vessy. [12]

"I think our role," he says, "is to become ever more sensitive to cultural concerns and to represent all different points of view, reflecting cultural and political concerns whenever possible and appropriate. It's not our business to advocate any particular political or economic agenda. Our main goal is to report the news as factually, accurately, and timely as possible. Our kind of journalism is often not practiced elsewhere in the world, even in sophisticated Western democracies. TV frequently is used as a social or political instrument. Our standards of journalism indicate that we are not advocates. That, in itself, helps us overcome some of the natural barriers that exist because we are Americans and represent Western culture. [13] Vesey used the Persian Gulf War to illustrate hes point, indicating that CNN International's programs included the full range of Arab opinion, including comment from a number of states that were not protagonists in the dispute but had political and cultural concerns.

Satellite television does cause cultural concerns in a number of developing countries. As summarized by Vesey, "There's just a political feel in many developing countries that ideas, unchecked, are a dangerous thing. Whether they are contrary to the religion or contrary to the political order, it's felt that they could have a subversive influence.

"For these countries, changes are occurring. Not only is CNN International available, but Asia-Sat and others will bring entertainment programming. In India there is concern that perhaps CNN International might impose a consumer-oriented value system on a country, a religion, and a society that is, in many ways, very happily closed to the outside world in order to protect its way of thinking and its way of life. In China, the technology is not in place to deliver very much programming, but political concerns result in opposition to global programming. Pakistan relies on the use of electronic black blocks to chase female figures around the TV screen and spare the viewer the spectacle of Western dress. There is no attempt to censor the information—no dropping, editing, or adding materials. They simply block some of the visuals. Malaysia, identifying the source of the problem, banned the sale of satellite receivers. Sales are restricted in Thailand. Indonesia allowed the distribution of satellite dishes at a time when few programs existed for domestic consumption.

"In almost every case, the countries are having to reevaluate their thoughts on these matters. They understand that they cannot control, as they once did, the broadcast signals coming into their country. They are bowing to the inevitable; but with some reluctance and a great deal of concern." [14]

Another cultural concern is the differences in styles used by persons from different parts of the globe. Boston WGBH staff Alain Jehlan describes some of the sit-

uations he has encountered. "If a program is designed to show style differences, then people don't mind variations, but if the objective is to produce a seamless show—without indication of which co-producer did which part—then one needs to be mindful of commonly used different approaches. For example, Russian productions sometimes seem chaotic or confusing to Americans. It's just that they are structured differently. They use a spiral approach. They make once around on story and then come back and deepen it. Its beautiful and emotional, but in the U.S. you get confused, because we're used to more a linear style. British satire is very popular, but many Americans prefer programs that are more sentimental. German documentaries tend to emphasize straightforward lecture with less focus on human interest vignettes. Japanese programs may emphasize what's up and coming, in contrast to an American style that may be more questioning: 'Is this a good idea, or not?' Also, Japanese programs may use more narration, while Americans prefer to use more people on camera. In any event, language, the most frequently mentioned problem of international co-production, can be the least of the problems in planning a viable cross-cultural co-production that will satisfy the audience for whom it is intended."[15]

ABC's Lydia Stephans highlights yet another aspect of the cultural challenges in co-production. Her situation of working with the Cubans on the Pan American Games is similar to working with many of the developing countries that rely on centralized decisionmaking. "Some pretty stressed-out New Yorkers thought their life and their career were on the line when something wasn't done as quickly as they needed to do it. But the New Yorker style must accommodate the Cuban style, and the government procedures. Appearing with their laundry list of needs and saying 'do-it-do-it' didn't work. First of all, the meetings began when people got there—not synchronized to the second digital clock appointment time. Second, Cubans operate completely differently from the way we do. When someone from ABC goes somewhere, they are responsible for making the decisions for their department; the Cuban organization representatives are not responsible. They must take everything back to the Central Committee. So from the smallest request to the most major decision, people had no authority to make decisions; they could only communicate it to the Central Committee, wait for an answer, and then get back to us."[16]

Dress code can also be a cultural block in some places. Herb Fuller notes that Madeira has been a tourist culture for more than 500 years. The tourists are nearly naked. The natives wear long pants and shirts buttoned to the top. Even among the tourists, the standards vary depending on the time of day. "One British dowager smugly commented that the place was simply disintegrating because these people want to come into restaurants without ties. But a half day later, she could be seen topless at the pool."[17] Consider with whom you will be doing business before you dress for the day. In what environment? Dress in a manner that does not make your appearance more of an issue than the subject matter of your conversation. Take a jacket and tie or the female version thereof. Learn the Halloween principle: there's a costume for every occasion.

Language, while easier to deal with than some of these less quantifiable cultural judgments, does present challenges in international co-production. Certainly English is increasingly acceptable. English has become the common language for scientific and business transactions, and for many, the neutral language. Thanks to

the colonialism of the 19th century, English is already a second language in many parts of the world. But by and large only a segment of any country speaks English as a second language. For example, the former Soviet Union has some 70 languages and dialects. Consider the audience for your production. If you want to reach across all the language barriers within a country as diverse as the Soviet Union, it almost requires program distribution by cassette in each of the appropriate languages.

From a foreigner's point of view, American culture biases production too. To quote the EBU's Pierre Brunel-Lantenac, "I do believe the Americans are a bit too much sons of Hollywood—well done and beautiful—even for their news coverage."[18] Again, one must assess the prospective audience. Communicating in the actual language spoken might not be enough. One must also use the style of language that is understood in a given geographic location.

Chauvinism is another aspect of cultural concerns, especially American and, to some extent, West European chauvinism. Meg Gottemoeller describes the following conversation with a Malaysian woman who asked, "How would you like it if a film crew from Malaysia came to Germany and did a film for the world on German pollution problems? The third world is always treated as receivers—rather than producers—of material." Gottemoeller went on to describe a conversation with a group of Asians who had agreed to participate in a co-production with Europeans. But the Asians wondered why Asians should only listen to Europeans.[19]

If you are an American considering co-production, test out your biases the same way you would test for racism or sexism. Substitute the other nationality, race, sex, politics, values, or religion for yours in the discussion and see whether or not the proposition still sounds equitable and reasonable to pursue.

TECHNOLOGY

The rapid changes in our global neighborhood are greatly influenced by the rapid changes in technology. Television first came to the public in low definition broadcast in Berlin in 1935, in high definition standards through the BBC in London in 1936, in Moscow in 1938, and in the United States in a higher definition standard in 1941. World War II interfered with everyone's work. But during the 1950s more than 50 countries inaugurated television. It wasn't until the 1980s, however, that television really shrank the size of the globe with the widespread use of live satellite transmission.[20] In addition to satellite availability, fiber optics and interactive programming are transforming communications as we enter the new century. The new types of equipment known to any professional in the field have also made it far easier to shoot footage in remote situations and under a wide range of circumstances. A few technological realities have not changed, however. The person involved in international co-production has no choice but to deal with format differences throughout the world and with electrical current differences. Let's look at how technology affects co-production.

Formats

Three different video formats are common worldwide. The international television producer needs to know whether the format used by the prospective audience

differs from the format of the equipment to be used while making the production. They are:

- National Television System Committee (NTSC) is the name of the format used in the United States, initially for black and white scan rates and later for color. It is principally used in North and South America and Japan.
- Phase Alternate Line (PAL) is the name for the German color television system. It is used in many European countries.
- Sequence Couleur a Memoire (SECAM) is the French color television system used also in the former Soviet Union, the former Eastern bloc countries, and a number of Middle East and African countries.

Consult Figure 5 to note which format is used where you plan to film a production, *and* which format is used by your prospective audience. If you need to convert to another format after the production is complete, consult the facilities in your area. One sample price schedule is shown in Figure 6. It is used by one company in New York City. Prices will vary depending on the quality of the equipment used to make the conversion, the market in the particular city, and the demand for this type of service.

Note that frequently in Europe, and occasionally in other places, one can find a video player and an accompanying monitor that has the ability to play any one of the three formats. For widespread use, however, the master tape should be available in the format common in the country where it is to be shown.

For live programming like a Space Bridge—two way live—two cameras are at each end as a rule, each using its own format. In each studio one needs both up- and downlink satellite capability. In addition, one needs, at both ends, the ability to convert the signal for the receiving audience.

Electrical Current

One of the most exasperating aspects of international production is dealing with the differences in electrical current in different countries. You not only need the right power converters but to make sure that, once converted, you are operating at the right frequency for your equipment. Products designed for use in the United States conform to the American electrical service and operate at 60 hertz, but much of the rest of the world operates at 50 hertz. Hertz measures the frequency of the electricity in cycles per second. You need to operate at the proper voltage—120 or 240. Voltage measures the units of electromotive force of the electricity. Equipment might not work if operated on the wrong current, or worse, equipment might be damaged. You also need to be able to operate on batteries without power—usually a necessity in some phase of an international production.

Producer Eric Johnston adds, "Lighting also requires special attention when dealing with equipment designed for use with different electrical currents. For example, European current differs from American. One simply uses converters with the American equipment so that it can function on European power. But if there are fluorescent lights in the shoot, or if you are videotaping slides, arrange to use lights and projectors manufactured for the same cycle current for which your television

LINES/FIELDS	COLOR	VOLTAGE (V)	FREQUENCY (Hz)	Country
625/50	PAL	220	50	AFGHANISTAN
625/50		220	50	ALBANIA
625/50	PAL	127-220	50	ALGERIA
625/50		220	50	ANDORRA
625/50		220	50	ANGOLA
625/50	PAL N	220	50	ARGENTINA
625/50	PAL	240	50	AUSTRALIA
625/50	PAL	220	50	AUSTRIA
625/50	PAL	220	50	AZORES
525/60	NTSC	120	60	BAHAMAS
625/50	PAL	220	50	BAHRAIN
625/50	PAL		50	BANGLADESH
525/60	NTSC		50	BARBADOS
625/50	PAL	120	50	BELGIUM
525/60	NTSC	120	60	BERMUDA
525/60	NTSC	115-230	60	BOLIVIA
525/60	PAL M	220	60	BRAZIL
625/50	SECAM	220	50	BULGARIA
625/50		220	50	BURUNDI
625/50		220	50	CAMEROON
525/60	NTSC	120-240	60	CANADA
625/50	PAL	127	50	CANARY IS.
625/50		220	50	CENTRAL AFRICAN REP.
625/50		230	50	CEYLON
625/50		220	50	CHAD
525/60	NTSC	220	50	CHILE
625/50	PAL	220	50	CHINA (PEOPLES REP)
525/60	NTSC	120-220	60	COLOMBIA
625/50	SECAM	220	50	CONGO (PEOPLES REP)
525/60	NTSC	110	60	COSTA RICA
525/60	NTSC	120	60	CUBA
525/60	NTSC	120	60	CURACAO
625/50	PAL	220	50	CYPRUS
625/50	SECAM	220	50	CZECHOSLOVAKIA
625/50		220	50	DAHOMEY
625/50	PAL	220	50	DENMARK
525/60	NTSC	110	60	DOMINICAN REP.
525/60	NTSC	120	60	ECUADOR
625/50	SECAM	220	50	EGYPT
525/60	NTSC	110	60	EL SALVADOR
625/50		127	50	ETHIOPIA
625/50		240	50	FIJI
625/50	PAL	220	50	FINLAND
625/50	SECAM	115-230	50	FRANCE
625/50	SECAM	127-220	50	GABON
625/50			50	GAMBIA
625/50	SECAM	220	50	GERMANY (DEM REP)
625/50	PAL	220	50	GERMANY (FED. REP)
625/50		230	50	GHANA
625/50	PAL	230	60	GIBRALTAR
625/50	PAL	127-220	50	GREAT BRITAIN

LINES/FIELDS	COLOR	VOLTAGE (V)	FREQUENCY (Hz)	Country
625/50	SECAM	110-220	50	GREECE
525/60	NTSC	220	50	GREENLAND
525/60	NTSC	110	60	GUAM
525/60	SECAM	110-220	60	GUATEMALA
625/50	SECAM	127	50	GUINEA
625/50	SECAM	115-220	50	GUYANA
525/60	SECAM	115-220	60	HAITI
525/60	NTSC	117	60	HAWAII
525/60	NTSC	110-220	60	HONDURAS
625/50	PAL	220	50	HONG KONG
625/50	SECAM	220	50	HUNGARY
625/50	PAL	220	50	ICELAND
625/50	PAL	230	50	INDIA
625/50	PAL	220	50	INDONESIA
625/50	SECAM	220	50	IRAN
625/50	SECAM	220	60	IRAQ
625/50	PAL	220	50	IRELAND
625/50	PAL	230	50	ISRAEL
625/50	PAL	127-220	50	ITALY
625/50	SECAM	220	50	IVORY COAST
625/50	PAL	110	60	JAMAICA
525/60	NTSC	100-200	50,60	JAPAN
625/50	PAL	220	50	JORDAN
625/50	PAL	240	50	KENYA
625/50			50	KOREA (NORTH)
525/60	NTSC	100	60	KOREA (SOUTH)
625/50	PAL	240	50	KUWAIT
625/50	SECAM	110-190	50	LEBANON
625/50	PAL	120	60	LIBERIA
625/50	SECAM	120	50	LIBYA
625/50	SECAM	120-208	50	LUXEMBOURG
625/50		127-220	50	MALAGASY REP.
625/50		220	50	MALAWI
625/50	PAL	240	50	MALAYSIA
625/50		125	50	MALI
625/50		240	50	MALTA
625/50	SECAM	127	60	MARTINIQUE
625/50		220	50	MAURETANIA
625/50	SECAM	220	50	MAURITIUS
525/60	NTSC	127-220	60	MEXICO
625/50	NTSC	125	50,60	MONACO
625/50			50	MONGOLIA
625/50	SECAM	115	50	MOROCCO
625/50	PAL	220	50	MOZAMBIQUE
625/50	PAL	220	50	NETHERLANDS
525/60	NTSC	120-220	60	NETHERLANDS ANTILLES
625/50	SECAM	220	50	NEW CALEDONIA
625/50	PAL	230	50	NEW ZEALAND
525/60	NTSC	117	60	NICARAGUA
625/50	NTSC	220	50	NIGER (REP)

LINES/FIELDS	COLOR	VOLTAGE (V)	FREQUENCY (Hz)	Country
625/50	PAL	220	50	NIGERIA
625/50	PAL	230	50	NORWAY
625/50	PAL	220	50	OMAN
625/50	PAL	220	60	PAKISTAN
525/60	NTSC	110	60	PANAMA
625/50	PAL	220	60	PARAGUAY
525/60	NTSC	220	60	PERU
525/60	NTSC	115	60	PHILIPPINES
625/50	SECAM	220	60	POLAND
625/50	PAL	220	50	PORTUGAL
525/60	NTSC	120	60	PUERTO RICO
625/50	PAL	220	50	RHODESIA
625/50	PAL	220	50	RUMANIA
625/50	SECAM	220	50	RWANDA
525/60		120	60	SAMOA
625/50	SECAM	125	50	SAUDI ARABIA
625/50	SECAM	127	50	SENEGAL
625/50	PAL	230	50.60	SIERRA LEONE
625/50	PAL	230	50	SINGAPORE
625/50		220	50	SOMALIA (REP OF)
625/50	PAL	220	50	SOUTH AFRICA
625/50	PAL	127-220	50	SPAIN
625/50			50	SPANISH SAHARA
525/60	NTSC	220	60	ST. KITTS
625/50	PAL	240	50	SUDAN
525/60	NTSC	115-127	50	SURINAM
625/50	PAL		50	SWAZILAND
625/50	PAL	220	50	SWEDEN
625/50	PAL	220	50	SWITZERLAND
625/50	SECAM	115-220	50	SYRIA
625/50	SECAM		50	TAHITI
525/60	NTSC	100	60	TAIWAN
625/50	PAL	230	50	TANZANIA
625/50	PAL	220	50	THAILAND
625/50		127-220	50	TOGOLESE REP.
525/60	NTSC	117	60	TRINIDAD & TOBAGO
625/50	SECAM	117-220	50	TUNISIA
625/50	PAL	110-220	50	TURKEY
625/50	PAL	220	50	UGANDA
625/50		220	50	UPPER VOLTA
625/50	PAL	220	50	URUGUAY
525/60	NTSC	110	60	U.S.A.
625/50	SECAM	220	50	C.I.S. (U.S.S.R.)
525/60	NTSC	110-220	60	VENEZUELA
525/60	NTSC	120	60	VIETNAM
525/60	NTSC	115	60	VIRGIN IS.
625/50			50	YEMEN
625/50	PAL	220	50	YUGOSLAVIA
625/50	SECAM	220	50	ZAIRE
625/50	SECAM	230	50	ZAMBIA

▶ *Figure 5 World Video Standards. (Source: Devlin Company, 150 W. 55th St., New York, N.Y. 10019. Many other companies also handle conversions.)*

Sample Format Conversion Costs

■ "SUPER D-SCAN" STANDARDS CONVERSION

	QUANTITY	SPOT	5:00	15:00	30:00	45:00	60:00	90:00	120:00	
HIGH BAND / HIGH BAND	1	$115	$140	$150	$250	$350	$420	$600	$700	M-II, D2 PAL
Including D2, 2", 1"C, BETACAM,	2	95	104	125	208	291	349	498	581	and 2",
BETA SP, 3/4" SP and M-II	3	86	94	113	188	263	315	450	525	add $150
(Stock included for SPOT only)	4	78	85	102	170	238	285	408	476	interface
	5+	70	76	92	153	214	256	366	427	charge
HIGH BAND / LOW BAND	1	$90	$100	$125	$195	$265	$325	$400	$550	M-II, D2 PAL
(Stock included)	2	75	83	104	162	220	270	332	457	and 2",
	3	68	75	94	146	199	244	300	413	add $150
	4	61	68	85	133	180	221	272	374	interface
	5+	55	61	76	119	161	198	244	336	charge
LOW BAND / LOW BAND	1	$70	$85	$115	$150	$205	$230	$300	$350	
(Stock included)	2	58	71	95	125	170	191	249	291	
	3	51	64	86	112	154	173	225	263	
	4	48	58	78	102	139	156	204	238	
	5+	43	52	70	92	125	140	183	214	

SELECTED TAKES AND/OR REEL CHANGES: $10 each   **INSERT EDIT (CLEAN):** $25 each   **ASSEMBLE EDIT (CRASH):** $15 each

■ DUPLICATION

	QUANTITY	SPOT		QUANTITY	15:00	30:00	60:00	90:00	120:00	
HIGH BAND NTSC	1	$35		1	$40	$75	$150	$225	$300	D2, add $10
Including D2, 2", 1"C,	2-6	27		2	33	62	125	187	249	M-II, D2 PAL,
BETACAM, BETA SP,	7-20	23		3	30	56	113	169	225	and 2",
3/4" SP and M-II	21-50	16		4	27	51	102	153	204	add $150
(Stock included)	51-100	13		5+	24	46	92	137	183	interface
	100+	upon request				(Stock not included)				charge
HIGH BAND PAL / SECAM	1	$55		1	$70	$100	$200	$300	$400	
	2	50		2	60	75	150	225	300	
(Stock included)	3	45		3	50	70	140	210	260	
	4	40		4	40	65	130	190	240	
	5+	upon request		5+	............upon request............					
						(Stock not included)				

	QUANTITY	10:00	20:00	30:00	60:00	75:00		QUANTITY	10:00	20:00	30:00	60:00	75:00	
3/4"	1	$31	$38	$45	$63	$97	**3/4"**	1	$40	$50	$60	$90	$120	From PAL/
NTSC	2-6	22	28	33	46	80	**PAL/SECAM**	2-6	30	35	40	60	110	SECAM
(Stock	7-20	21	26	31	43	66	(Stock included)	7-20	25	30	35	50	100	High Band,
included)	21-50	19	24	28	40	61		21-50	22	28	32	45	90	add $15
	51-100	18	22	26	37	56		51-100	20	25	30	40	80	
	100+	............upon request............						100+	............upon request............					

	QUANTITY	10:00	20:00	30:00	45:00	60:00	90:00	120:00	180:00	240:00	360:00	
VHS NTSC	1	$27	$32	$38	$44	$50	$68	$82	$96	$111	$157	
(Stock included)	2-6	18	22	26	32	38	50	67	84	102	150	
	7-20	16	20	23	27	32	35	55	76	96	137	
	21-50	14	17	19	20	22	29	42	55	70	96	
	51-100	12	14	15	17	19	20	31	45	57	76	
	100+	....................upon request....................										
VHS PAL/SECAM	1	$35	$45	$53	$63	$70	$95	$125	$145	$165	$235	From PAL/
(Stock included)	2-6	26	32	35	42	50	65	80	95	110	155	SECAM
	7-20	23	28	30	35	40	50	60	70	80	115	High Band,
	21-50	21	25	27	31	35	45	55	60	70	100	Add $15
	51-100	18	23	25	27	30	40	50	55	65	90	
	100+	....................upon request....................										

SELECTED TAKES AND/OR REEL CHANGES: $10 each   **INSERT EDIT (CLEAN):** $25 each   **ASSEMBLE EDIT (CRASH):** $15 each

▶ *Figure 6* (*Source: Devlin Company, 150 W. 55 St., New York, NY 10019. Many other companies also do conversions. One should compare prices.*)

equipment was designed. Otherwise, despite the converter used on some of the equipment, the flicker of the lights may be noticable in your video."[21]

Independent American producer Harry Munns describes his experience dealing with electrical currents while shooting a video in Moscow (Russia) and Tiblisi (Georgia), two parts of the former Soviet Union. "Many countries outside the U.S., including the U.S.S.R., use 220 volt/50 hertz current in residential and commercial

buildings. A little research would be advisable before deciding on a particular model of adapter. While a 110 volt hair dryer or Lowell lights might work just fine on voltage as high as 190 volts, sensitive electronic equipment like battery chargers and monitors cannot always tolerate voltage fluctuation. A phone call to the adapter manufacturer's engineering department could help avert problems that are not easily solved in the Soviet Union."[22]

Plugs are another booby trap of the technological era. One sometimes wonders how we're able to send astronauts to the moon but are unable to have easily available the right kind of electrical plug for the outlets of a given country. I recently experienced the electrical plug problem with equipment I purchased in the United States to be used in Holland. The equipment was purchased with an adapter for current adjustment, but the adapter had the type of plug used in England. The Dutch have another type of plug. I searched major metropolitan areas of the United States before I left for Europe and could only find plugs that would allow American cords to be used in outlets all over the world—none that would allow English cords to be used in Dutch outlets. But everyone assured me that this would be an easy item to find in Europe. I searched stores in major metropolitan areas of Holland, Germany, and Belgium and could easily find plugs that would allow their cords to be used in England, America, or any other part of the world, but none that would allow English (or American) cords to be used in their outlets. Finally, I found what I needed—in England.

Satellite Transmission

Space Bridges would not be possible without the satellite technology that has come into use since the late 1970s. Without this technology, electronic news gathering and cable television would not have reached their present state of development. International co-production would not have become a popular mode of production without the expansion of satellite because the concept of international cooperation would not have become a viable option for the typical producer.

Satellite brought cable television into millions of living rooms, simultaneously shrinking the size of the globe and expanding the size of the typical family's neighborhood. In 1977 there were about 12 million cable subscribers. In 1989, 122 transponders on 14 satellites carried cable TV. In 1989—thanks to the initiation of satellite distribution—there were more than 50 million subscribers.[23]

PBS was the first major broadcaster to test satellite use. In 1978 it began a point-to-multipoint (to affiliates throughout the country) transmission and found the experiment successful. Others climbed on board. First cable, then, by the end of 1984, all the major American networks, made the transition to satellite distribution.

The right to use a satellite transponder can be bought or leased. (A transponder is the unit within the satellite that receives and transmits signals. Each transponder handles a single program. Each satellite carries a number of transponders.) Originally, international television service was carried on Intelsat satellites and Comsat earth stations in the United States and government-owned earth stations in other countries. Intelsat is a system of satellites owned by a consortium of 108 countries. In recent years independent services have also begun, notably Pan Am Sat to South America and Orion Satellite to Europe.[24]

When purchasing satellite time, you must decide on several things. Do you want protected, unprotected, or preemptable time? Protected provides a backup satellite or transponder in case of service interruption. Unprotected has no backup. Preempted time is when the transponder is taken as a backup for someone else. Prices vary as expected. You also need to consider the period of service—an occasional hour or a long-term regular period. The long-term rates are better. Or perhaps you want to purchase the transponder or part of a transponder. Finally, you need to decide on the scope of service purchased. Does it include only the transponder, or does it also include the uplink and downlink services?[25]

Those interested in international transmission should contact Communication Satellite Corporation (COMSAT), World Systems Division, 950 L'Enfant Plaza S.W., Washington, DC 20024.

As of 1990 four satellite carriers were licensed by the FCC to own and operate satellites and offer their services for sale or lease. These are:

1. AT&T, Room 4C103, Bedminster, NJ 07921
2. GE American Communications, Inc., Four Research Way, Princeton, NJ 08540
3. GTE Spacenet Corp., 1700 Old Meadow Road, McLean, VA 22102
4. Hughes Communication, Inc., Box 92424, Los Angeles, CA 90009

Those interested in transmission in Alaska would contact Alascom, Inc., Box 6607, Anchorage, AK 99502.[26]

Fiber Optics

Satellites compete with microwave transmission, coaxial cable, and—the newest form of transmission—fiber optics. Utility companies are replacing the traditional coaxial cable with fiber optic cables as rapidly as possible. This new technology was first tested for video transmission in 1980. By 1991 some 300 cities in the United States were connected by fiber optic cables, and many specific corporate, government, and communication routes throughout the world are wired. Fiber technology can transmit high quality voice, data, image, and video in two-way communication at a cheaper rate and in a more accessible, more flexible manner than satellite transmission. In addition, privacy of transmission is possible. The customer using the fiber for video transmission won't have the mechanical worries of arranging the location, the equipment, and the satellite time; these mechanics will be built into the system.[27]

Already fiber is offering many advantages to the video producer:

- Studios are directly linked to satellite ground stations. No extra transport is required.
- Studios can be linked with other studios in a point to point communication, enabling a video back-and-forth that is helpful for business and helpful for the video producer collaborating with others.
- Television stations can regionalize their programs and advertising distribution to provide more flexibility for themselves and to create new revenue opportunities. This capability can, in turn, make it possible for producer

products that have a more specialized appeal not to be rejected but to be shown to segments of one's general audience.

- Full broadcasting quality videoconferencing can occur between national or international sites via telephone company equipment. There is no need for special equipment. The material can be transmitted via fiber or, if technology requires, via videotape or satellite up- and downlink.
- Instant video can be transmitted back and forth between locations that are wired, without the need for sending out a microwave truck. For example, TV stations can be wired directly to sports arenas, state capitols, and other locations to which they regularly send television crews.
- Soon a video dial tone service will be possible. One will simply go to a pay telephone, insert the payment required, and plug in one's camera to the jack provided. The picture will be transmitted to the intended party. Imagine the uses for unscheduled news events, for live entertainment interviews, for production crews, for videoconferencing, and for corporate training.
- Academic institutions can use fiber optic loops for distance learning—bringing one expert into a number of classrooms simultaneously, or bringing a classroom into a museum or laboratory, or enabling several classrooms of students to simultaneously participate in a common discussion.[28]

By the early years of the new century, the major remaining obstacle—installing the fiber—will be history, and the techniques used by video producers in the 1990s will be quite outdated.

Satellites rely on fixed point-to-point transmission, and fiber optics, using telephone lines, will be provide more versatile transmission. In addition, satellites age and outlive their usefulness, and, geosynchronous orbit parking spaces for satellites are limited.

Geographic and economic limitations still exist, however. One won't soon be able to use fiber optics to involve students from the across world in a program held, for example, in a Central American rain forest. The telephone lines don't exist. Much of the industrialized world, and many locations in the former Eastern bloc countries, will enjoy this global neighborhood form of communication before another decade passes. The remaining task then will be one of providing telephone lines to those parts of the world where people can't imagine that some of us consider this form of communication a necessity, no longer a luxury. Perhaps, however, you should produce your videos about the rain forest now; when the phone lines are finally in place, technology may have greatly altered a traditional culture.

Interactive Programming

The television professional planning to work in international production and co-production in the next two decades has a marvelous opportunity to create demonstration uses for interactive programming. Watching a half-hour or hour-long show may become boring when one can instead choose to interact with the event being watched—to learn or be entertained in the way that each individual finds most desirable. Corporate teleconferencing, news broadcasting, sporting events, educational

and documentary programming, even video publishing can be done in many new ways with interactive technology.

Many companies have developed means of integrating the video and the computer, and there are systems where you can plug your video signal into the computer and watch it on your computer screen. New in the market in the early 1990s are "computers with built-in CD-ROMs that can connect to your TV or home entertainment center, creating interactive learning options."[29] The combining of a computer disk (CD) with computer read only memory (ROM) has resulted in CD-ROM technology, a wafer that can hold the equivalent of 1,000 floppy disks—250,000 pages of text or 10,000 digitized still pictures—accessible instantly at any data point.

"You can do a lot with a touch-tone phone and a VCR—you could have 200,000 students taking one course," says Harry Lasker, an executive with Applied Learning International, a high-tech education and training corporation.[30] Lasker and his colleagues are combining interactive video with computers to provide one-on-one tutorials that use videodiscs. For example:

- A law student can learn about search and seizure through a videodisc drama.
- A single CD-ROM can provide an entire library of information in text and visual information on a given topic. It can allow one an interdisciplinary look at any topic—historical, artistic, literary, political, and technical—available in ways that no single professor or video documentary could make possible.
- CD-ROM technology allows the expertise of a world renowned professor to become the syllabus for students anywhere—not just at the institution where such person resides.
- Simulation learning is possible with this technology—place the person in the audience in the pilot's chair, in the driver's seat, as the surgeon in the operating room, in the control room of a nuclear reactor.
- Role-playing can become a unique teaching device. At Harvard School of Education, Mark L. Verheyden Hilliard developed an interactive program where the student learns the consequences of an individual's social and political decisions by playing the role of a person who lived in colonial America.

Interactive programming takes a quantum leap forward in the early 1990s because of two new products available in 1992. First, CDI—an interactive disc in compact disc format—can provide high quality audio, video, graphics, data, and text material. This new technology also represents a first in international standardization agreements in that products made by different manufacturers can be used interchangeably. Eric Johnston, whose firm, Johnston and Associates, does CDI, notes that "it is conceivable that well before the year 2000, CDI will be as popular as, or even replace, VHS videotape."[31] Sony and Phillips have taken leading roles in the technology development. Productions that combine video and computer can now be made easily available for the consumer market.

Just one example of the multitude of international television production possibilities is a project in development by Berlitz. Berlitz will sell a CDI that one can

play on a portable compact disc viewer while on an international trip and learn a language, see a map, plot a route, hear about (and see in detail) the places one is passing, and secure other travel information.

"CDI consumer players are reasonably priced, and some are the size of a portable CD player but include a four-inch video screen and a built-in mouse," says Johnston. "Sony's machine, called an Interactive Compact Disk Viewer, released in 1992, runs on batteries and can plug into any standard television set. Not only is the technology easily usable for the consumer, it's extremely useful for a producer with work in progress. Another feature of CDI technology useful to the producer is that the industrial machines can use NTSC, PAL, or SECAM formats simply by flipping a switch on the back of the machine."[32]

A new chip called a M-PEG, also released in 1992, enables producers of interactive video to secure full motion video and no longer be handicapped by the poorer quality video that resulted from the the compressed video technology used before 1992.

Interactive television has enormous possibilities for creating a global neighborhood of people who are informed about their area of interest, who all are empowered as participants in the decisionmaking for their own future and for their community. Unless we are to once again divide the world into haves and have nots, interactive technology must become a tool used by co-producers. U.S. Senator Albert Gore, who chairs the Senate Subcommittee on Science, Technology, and Space, comments, "We are witnessing the emergence of a truly global civilization based on shared knowledge in the form of digital code. The ability of nations to compete will depend on their ability to handle knowledge in this form."[33]

User Friendly Technology

"With the merger of television and computer technology, many new opportunities become available for the independent producer," comments producer Eric Johnston. "Nonlinear editing equipment is now readily available. With a computer mouse one can retrieve any segment at any point and not need to follow the time-consuming process of running the entire videotape. The Macintosh and DOS worlds are soon to be combined through an object-oriented linkage, making it much easier to create interactive programs from clients using two different data systems. The notebook PC with a cellular modem and an interactive video program will soon become as popular as the floppy disc or the VCR tape."[34]

Nonetheless, the bottom line for producers is summarized in a statement by former Harvard President Dereck Bok, who reminds those inclined to be fascinated with technology for technology's sake that "however people choose to communicate their ideas, it's the ideas that are important."[35]

Time to Assess

One of the most important impacts of the new communications technologies is the absence of any time to reflect. There's no time to carefully choose the words or the pictures. There's no time to evaluate how to place a message within its larger context. There's no time to determine whether or not misinterpretation is likely.

In the words of EBU's Pierre Brunel-Lantenac, "For us TV professionals, I

believe we must begin to examine how it is possible to work with the new technologies. And the technologies of the 1990s will soon be obsolete. In five years you'll carry the satellite uplink and your generators in your own two suitcases. But already, we have the possibility of translating immediately the reaction of our eye, and of trying to translate our emotion. If we work in a democratic press, we'll transmit immediately all the immediate events. What will be our responsibility. There's no time for reflection. You must broadcast instantly because the competition does the same. If after one or two hours you discover that this is not the reality, you have been manipulated and your public will have been deeply shocked. It was easier for the news reporter of the past. A release was written; time was allowed for editing, and the technological process was slower, thereby building in the safeguards that allowed for refining or altering one's first impressions."[36]

"And it is because of the new technologies that provide instant images in wartime that the pressure for news censorship grows. You had for the first time in the 1991 Persian Gulf War a situation where, because of satellite transmission, enemies could sit by their TV sets and watch the damage their weapons had caused their opponent. Never before."[37]

How do we handle press freedoms, the public's right to know, together with a nation's right to security and the expectation that the news will not broadcast distortions? Production and co-production with the new technologies on a shrunken globe pose new and important questions for the ethical television professional.

Notes

1. Personal interviews with Eric Johnston, President, Johnston and Associates, 265 Winter St., Waltham, MA 02154, tel.: 617-547-6612, December 4, 1990, and March 23, 1992.
2. Personal interview with Richard Sydenham, Producer, Special Programs Section, Department of Information, United Nations, Room S-955, New York, NY 10017, Fax: 212-963-4556, tel.: 212-963-6944.
3. Ibid.
4. Personal interview with Mary E. (Meg) Gottemoeller, President, World Information Corporation, 501 East 17th Street, Flatbush, Brooklyn, NY, tel.: 718-282-8027, December 16, 1990.
5. Personal interview with Tony Goodman, Deputy Director, IVCA, Bolsover House, 5/6 Clipstone St., London W1P 7EB, England, February 15, 1991.
6. Johnston interview.
7. Personal interview with Herb Fuller, independent filmmaker, 54 Preston Road, Somerville, MA 02143, August 13, 1991.
8. Teresa L. Waite, "As Networks Stay Home, Two Agencies Roam the World," *The New York Times,* Sunday, March 8, 1992, p. F5.
9. Sydenham interview. List used for workshop participants.
10. Fuller interview.
11. Ibid.
12. Telephone interview with Peter Vesey, Vice President, CNN International, One CNN Center, Atlanta, GA 30303, November 12, 1991.
13. Ibid.
14. Ibid.

15. Personal interview with Alain Jehlan, Director of Acquisitions, "Nova," WGBH, Boston, August 27, 1991.

16. Personal interview with Lydia Stephans, Director, Programming, ABC Sports, 47 West 66th Street, New York, NY 10023, tel.: 212-456-3702, August 23, 1991.

17. Fuller interview.

18. Personal interview with Pierre Brunel-Lantenac, Director, News Operations, European Broadcasting Union, Ancienne Route 17a/Casa Postale 67, CH-1218 Grand Saconnex, Geneva, Switzerland, Fax: 022-798-5897, tel.: 022-717-2821, February 22, 1991.

19. Gottemoeller interview.

20. Sidney W. Head, World Broadcasting Systems: A Comparative Analysis (Belmont, California: Wadsworth, 1985), p. 15

21. Johnston interview.

22. Harry Munns, "Shooting Through the Iron Curtain," *Videography,* (Videography, 2 Park Avenue, New York, NY 10016, tel.: 212-213-3444), May 1990, pp.31ff.

23. Andrew F. Inglis, *Satellite Technology,* (Stoneham, Mass.: Butterworth Heinemann/Focal Press, 1991), p. 17

24. Ibid., pp. 25–26.

25. Ibid., p. 86.

26. Ibid., pp. 84–85.

27. Presentation by Mitch Abel, Director of Video Transfer Services, New England Telephone Company, to the seminar sponsored by the Society of Motion Picture and Television Engineers and the Society of Broadcast Engineers, New England Telephone Company, 617-890-9999, October 9, 1991.

28. Ibid.

29. Craig Lambert, "The Electronic Tutor," *Harvard Magazine,* (Cambridge,Mass.: Harvard University, November-December 1990), p. 50.

30. Ibid., pp. 42–51.

31. Johnston interview.

32. Ibid.

33. Lambert, p. 51.

34. Johnston interview.

35. Lambert, p.50

36. Lantenac interview.

37. Ibid.

5

▼
▼
▼
▼
▼

Acquisition
and Distribution

Whatever is produced or co-produced has little value until it can be disseminated to its appropriate audience in order to inform, educate, or entertain. In order to know how buyers and sellers do business, the co-producer must understand (1) markets, (2) the ingredients of a successful transaction, and (3) how to pursue a particular acquisition transaction or arrange distribution.

THE WORLD MARKET

Successful marketing depends on knowing (1) what one's product is, (2) where one's audience is, and (3) how to use one's imagination to its full potential.

For example, if the audience is reached via broadcast television in a country where all television is state controlled, you need to approach it quite differently than if the audience is reached via broadcast television in a country where free market principles prevail. Similarly, if the product is entertainment (drama or sports), you will market it quite differently than if the product is news, a documentary, or an educational program.

The variations can become even more refined. New York independent distribution consultant Susan Ryan observes, "A lot of Europeans think that the only market in the U.S. is the Public Broadcasting System (PBS) or other broadcast or cable TV stations. In fact, The United States is different from most other countries in that there is a wide network of markets: colleges, libraries, and high schools that rent and buy films and tapes that you'd likely only see on TV in other countries. Also in the U.S. there is a much more developed specialized semi-theatrical market: museums, art galleries, university film centers where there are open showings, whether paid or free. And America has a wider range of alternative theaters that will show independent films and videos.

"The only countries I know (outside the United States) with a substantial educational market are England, Australia, and New Zealand. In Latin America, for example, an educational market does not exist, principally because it has not been customary to incorporate film and video into the curriculum. That's needed before you can have a market."[1]

In developing countries, finances and access to equipment and trained personnel are often hard to find. Consequently, it's no surprise that there are fewer

hours of programming, fewer channels, and less diversity in programming. This translates into a greater willingness to accept all sorts of tape produced abroad. If a station were to try to program something other than studio programs with 'talking heads' or the cheapest of syndicated movies, it might well follow the procedures South American channels used in receiving some of the 1991 Pan American Games. In that case, the host broadcasters, the Cubans, fed out a one hour package showing the highlights of the day—10 minutes of gymnastics, 15 minutes of baseball, and so on. If a particular country, say Brazil, had a request for a particular full game, they fed that also. However, reports indicate that none of the other countries was taking live programming from Cuba.[2]

One new component of the world market for the co-producer to consider is video publishing. The common availability of video cassette recorders by the late 1980s suddenly created a whole new method for video distribution, before available only to schools and institutions. Renting and buying video cassettes is in vogue. There's not a town square in America in the early 1990s without a video rental store. There's not a public market in a developing country without some would-be entrepreneur selling his or her sack full of videos.

In the decade ahead, one can expect creative producers and co-producers to take advantage of video publishing. It's an ideal distribution route to specialized markets, for special interest productions, for limited number sales—perhaps limited numbers available in a certain language, or for short-term markets, such as the audience from a particular sporting event. Video publishing can, but it doesn't have to, totally bypass traditional distribution through television broadcast stations or institutional outlets. The skill tapes produced by the BBC spin-off Educational Broadcasting Services Trust illustrate one use for video publishing—to distribute tapes for educational institutions to use with students.

The task for you as the co-producer is to identify video distributors in your area accessible to your audience and to determine what the best financial incentive would be for cooperative work. Will the distributors finance a production? Commission a tape? Will they only sign a more traditional distribution contract? Do you, as co-producer, want to embark upon distributing your own product?—a huge task if you don't have a captive market, the administrative and staff support to handle it, and the marketing expertise to get the greatest benefit for the least cost.

NEGOTIATING DISTRIBUTION CONTRACTS

Before it's possible to market one's co-production, it's necessary to have one's own house in legal order. Think through with a lawyer any legal problems before negotiating a distribution contract. What contract terms would be most beneficial? What questions must be raised during negotiation discussions?

Co-productions can present difficulties for a distributor because it usually is more complicated to deal with two or more parties than it is to complete a deal with one entity. Because the rights for distribution have important financial consequences, especially in potentially lucrative markets like the United States, each of the parties involved in the co-production may want to preserve her or his right to

negotiate for and receive specific profits to be received from distribution of the production.

Distribution contracts can involve other legal matters also. For example, labor unions are provided certain rights through their contracts, and there may be a need to obtain certain clearances before something produced in another labor market is viewed. For example, British Television produced "28 Up" for TV. The BBC never anticipated that it would have a large theatrical audience, but it did. There were significant legal problems in trying to clear that film for theatrical audiences in United States.

Always be careful with any contract to spell out how the costs will be allocated. Many costs are involved in product sales and distribution—the costs for distribution prints, for personnel, for advertising, for travel, and for postage, phone, and fax. Is the distributor being paid for each itemized cost, or are costs taken off the top of the profits as a percentage? If a percentage is agreed to, will the contract be a 50-50 split between the distributor and the film- or videomaker? Or will it be a 75-25 deal, where all costs are taken out of the distributor's end and the filmmaker gets a flat 25%? In a 75-25 split, the producer's advantage is not having to worry about anything, but the disadvantage is having less control over how advertising money is spent. For example, your product may end up only in a once-a-year mailing—no specialized treatment. Weigh how much control you want to have over distribution: how much money is spent, how the film or video is marketed, how many mailings are sent, and where they go. Sometimes a producer gets involved in a new project and just wants to turn the completed one over to a distributor. Sometimes the producer wants to be very involved.

Keep in mind that the more money you have, the more you will be able to control your marketing. Know whether you are negotiating in a buyer's or a seller's market. Know your self-interest—your sales objective. Know your distributor's self-interest—securing the maximum sales revenue from the most accessible markets. Know how to mesh these self-interests so that your distributer is more a partner than an adversary.

When a producer negotiates a distribution contract, it is important to know something about successful marketing in order to know what to request. Obviously, the more that can be spent on exposing people to the production, the more likely that it will be a success—assuming that it is a quality product, of course. It's essential for the production to be in a catalogue. Catalogues go to audiovisual centers and libraries and are used as references. Catalogues are especially important to advertise video productions that are appropriate for the educational market. But a producer should also push for the distributor to do specialized mailings—to target groups (e.g., unions, religious groups) and to institutions with large memberships (e.g., universities, school systems, civic organizations, museums). Mailings to specific individuals are best. In selecting a distributor, check what else the company has actually distributed to be sure that it has a certain number of customers who buy or rent the kind of program being distributed. Will this distributor be aggressive in marketing the product? How? If it does a package mailing, know what else is in the package. Such collaborative advertising will cut the cost for each party involved. Remember,

however, that at some point the benefit of being part of a successful package is offset by the disadvantage of being lost in the crowd.[3]

ACQUISITION AND DISTRIBUTION MODELS

The models discussed in the following sections present different modes of buying and selling—some are transactions between large institutions and some involve small entrepreneurs. The most important factor to remember in reading these models is that while making the best use of conventional approaches, never allow your imagination to conform to the models already tested. Simply use them as a launch pad. As the globe shrinks, the economy changes, markets shift, the technological tools increase, and your possibilities expand dramatically.

Institutional Nontheatrical (Documentary and Educational) Acquisition and Distribution

First, how does a public television network buy and sell programs? "Nova", the PBS science documentary program originating through WGBH TV in Boston, provides one model for nontheatrical marketing. Director of Acquisitions Alain Jelhan explains, "People we know we just keep in touch with and they send us proposals all the time. We get 300 proposals a year, easily. Just about everybody in U.S. who is making a film that could be suitable for 'Nova', knows about us and we don't have to go looking for them. They'll come to us unless they sell to National Geographic. In England that's also true for the majority of producers of our type of documentary.

"In other countries, where they don't know about us, matches sometimes develop from contacts made at television festivals or markets. There's a whole series of television markets that happen every year. The biggest one is called Marche Internationale de Programmes de Television, or MIP. [MIP-TV, Palais des Festivals, Cannes, France.] It's held each spring in Cannes, France, with emphasis on buying and selling syndicated programs. Thousands of producers, distributors, and TV station representatives come there every year. Goods are displayed in a booth. There are buyers wandering around. We at 'Nova' are buyers. Our programs also are sold there, but we have a distributor who does the selling. We wander around and look for things that might be interesting to buy. There are many other marketplaces and festivals [see the additional references in this chapter and in Chapter 6]. These places are expensive for the seller—especially for independent producers who want to sell. They are cheap for the buyers. The last one I went to for 'Nova' was in Marseilles and the market sponsors paid my plane fare and hotel. The sellers must pay large sums for their booth, and that's a principal source of the money to cover costs for the event and to bring in those of us who are the buyers.[4]

There are people set up in these markets who handle just documentaries. Because there's so much drama programming, it's hard sometimes to find the documentaries.

Jehlan continues, "At such a market, someone from 'Nova' met the fundraising producer whose company included the man who was producing the condor film. The result was that we bought into our co-production with him. Now, we just

keep in touch. We don't need the market, except that it's a good place to meet and catch up once a year."[5]

The United Nations provides another model for nontheatrical acquisition and distribution. U.N. Producer Richard Sydenham explains, "Looking at international production from the U.N. point of view is rather specific because our task is to publicize things that the U.N. does. Our work program is set in advance—part of the biennial budget cycle. The ideas for programs come up through the various committees of the General Assembly and then are finally formulated in the overall information program, voted on by the General Assembly for two years hence. For example, at the moment our work is focused on a major conference on environment and development held in Brazil in 1992. So we do programs on the relationship between environment and development and the myriad of subtopics.

"We distribute inhouse. We have sixty-five to seventy information centers in capitals around the world. Their job when they get our cassette is to get it onto local TV, into schools, shown to groups, etc. It involves 200 to 300 cassettes in at least English, French, and Spanish. For the Brazil conference we'll do Portuguese as well. We make cassettes here and send them in all the different TV standards."[6]

The United Nations also has contracts with educational distributors, especially for North America, where there's a tremendous amount of product and it's difficult to get it on TV. Journal Film, Sterling, and California News Reel are some of the educational distributors with whom the U.N. has contracts. They also use Cinema Guild and Marlin in Canada for non-TV distribution. They make the cassette and the U.N. gets a cut of the profit.

Some of the distributors of documentary and educational film and video programs are listed in Figure 7, followed by a listing of documentary television distributors. Many, but not all, of those listed distribute U.N. video material.

The United Nations is now finishing a school series called "About the United Nations." It has done programs on apartheid, Palestine, Africa recovery, decolonization, literacy, and in 1992 is doing a program on the environment and development and one on human rights, with emphasis on children's rights. The programs are designed specifically for high school and college. The U.N. orients its work to a general audience, but it often uses a young person to present the topic. Issues can be dense and complicated. The U.N. also does an educational study guide to go with the TV cassettes. Most of these programs have not yet been on cable or broadcast because the distribution program is just in the development phase.

The U.N. women's literacy program provides another example of distribution strategy. United Nations Producer Richard Sydenham states, "I shot 12 hours in Mali, and barely 7–8 minutes ended up in the women's literacy program. I'd like to make two or three other short programs. I'll use some for 'U.N. in Action' that becomes a segment of CNN World Report. I'll try to get Discovery Channel money to make another program."[7]

The U.N. also advertises for co-production partners, indicating that the level of co-production ranges from "seed money to co-sponsorship, and can include exchanges of footage or camera crews, and use of archives or facilities. Reciprocal arrangements range from screen credits to shared distribution rights."[8]

(Note: International code precedes all telephone numbers except the U.S. and Canada. If calling the U.S. from another country, put a 1 in front of the telephone or fax number.) Publications identified in Chapter 6 will provide additional listings.

- Journal Films, Inc., 930 Pitner, Evanston, IL 60202, U.S.A., tel.: 800-323-5448
- Sterling Educational Films, 241 E. 34th Street, New York, NY 10016, U.S.A., tel.: 212-779-0202
- California Newsreel, 630 Natoma Street, San Francisco, CA 94103, U.S.A., tel.: 415-621-6196
- Cinema Guild, Division of Document Associates, 1697 Broadway, New York, NY 10019, U.S.A., tel.: 212-246-5522.
- Barr Films, Inc., 12801 Schabarum, P.O. Box 7878, Irwindale, CA 91706-7878, U.S.A., tel.: 800-234-7878.
- Great Plains National Instructional Television Library, P.O. 80669, University of Nebraska, Lincoln, NE 68501-0669, U.S.A., tel.: 800-228-4630.
- First Run/Icarus Films, Inc., 153 Waverly Place, New York, NY 10014, U.S.A., tel.: 800-876-1710.
- Lucerne Media, 37 Ground Pine Road, Morris Plains, NJ 07905, U.S.A., tel.: 800-341-2293.
- National Black Programming Consortium, Inc., 1266 East Broad Street, One-East, Columbus, OH 43205, U.S.A., tel.: 614-252-0921.
- The Video Project, 5332 College Ave., Suite 101, Oakland, CA 94618, U.S.A., tel.: 800-4-PLANET. This organization distributes films and videos advocating a safe and sustainable world.
- Focal Communications Pty. Ltd., 33 Chandas Street, St. Leonards, Sydney, NSW, Australia 2065, tel.: 61-2-437-6855.
- International Catholic Organization for Cinema and Audiovisual, rue de l'Orme, 8, B-1040 Brussels, Belgium, tel.: 32-2-734-42-94.
- Wereldmediatheek, Kerkstraat 150, 2008 Antwerp, Belgium.
- Globo Video, Sistema Globo de Video, Communicacao Ltda., Rue Ana Guimaraes 20, Rocha, Rio de Janeiro, RJ, Brazil.
- Marlin Motion Pictures, Ltd., Suite 200, 211 Watline Ave., Mississauga, Ontario, Canada, L4Z 1P3, tel.: 416-890-1500.
- Carrefour International, 6865 Christophe Colombe, Suite 307, Montreal, Quebec H2S 2H3, Canada, tel.: 514-272-2247.
- National Film Board of Canada, P.O. Box. 6100, Montreal, H3C 3H5, Canada.
- Visual Education Centre, 75 Horner Avenue, Unit One, Toronto, Ontario M8Z 4X5, Canada, tel.: 416-252-5907.
- Infor Film Servis, Stepanska 42, 11000 Prague 1, Czechoslovakia, tel.: 42-2-26-64-61.
- Statens Filmcentral, Verstergade 27, DK-1456, Copenhagen K, Denmark.
- Valtion Audiovisuaalinen Keskus, Hagnasgatan 2, SF-00530, Helsinki 53, Finland.
- Cinethque, 130 rue de Courcelles, 75017 Paris, France, tel.: 33-13-42-67-37-42.
- Context Film GMBH, Schleissheimerstrasse 180, 8000 Munchen 40, Germany, tel.: 49-89-307-1069, fax: 49-89-308-3721.
- Institut fur Film und Bild, Bavaria Film Platz 3, 8022 Grunwald, Germany, tel.: 49-30-8-01-50-76.
- Matthias Film, Gansheidestrasse 67, D-7000 Stuttgart 1, Germany, tel.: 49-711-24-04-10.
- Bharat Educational Media, 59 Kodambakkam High Road, North T. Nagar, Madras 600017, India.

(continued)

▶ *Figure 7* *Some Distributors of Documentary and Educational Programs. Publications identified in Chapter 6 will provide additional listings.*

- Studio Esse-PI, S.R.I., Via Modigliani, 20, 00147 Rome, Italy, tel.: 39-6-51-10-112.
- Educational Media, Inc., c/o Asahi Building, 6-7 Ginza 6-Chome, Chuo-Ku, Tokyo, Japan, tel.: 81-3-571-9351-5.
- Peliculas Mel, S.A., Urupan 17, 3er Piso, Mexico City 7 D.F., Mexico, tel.: 52-5-533-6616.
- Stichting Film en Wetenschap, Hengeveldstraat 29, Post Bus 9550, 35506 GN Utrecht, The Netherlands.
- Media Services N.Z., 28 Upland Street, Tauranga, New Zealand, tel.: 64-75-67-319.
- Statens Filmsentral, Schwensens Gate 6, N-Oslo 1, Norway.
- Filmo AB, Stromsatragrand 10, S-127 35 Skarholmen, Stockholm, Sweden, tel.: 46-8-97-04-30.
- Sol Film, Klara 0.12, S-105 33 Stockholm, Sweden.
- Concord Video and Film Council, Ltd., 201 Felixsrowe Road, Ipswich, Suffolk IP3 9BJ, United Kingdom, tel.: 44-473-726012.
- Contemporary Films Ltd., 24 Southwood Lawn Road, London N6 5SF, United Kingdom, tel.: 44-1-340-5715.
- Educational Media International, 235 Imperial Drive, Rayners Lane, Harrow, Middlesex HA2 7HE, United Kingdom, tel.: 44-1-868-1908; fax: 44-1-868-1991.
- Coe Film Associates, Inc., 65 E. 96th St., New York, NY 10128, U.S.A., tel.: 212-831-5355.
- Cinema Video Distributors, Ltd., 321 West 44th St., Suite 907A, New York, NY 10036, U.S.A., tel.: 212-246-3229. Distributes worldwide except the United States and Canada.
- Contemporary Films, Ltd., 24 Southwood Lawn Road, London N6 5SF, United Kingdom, tel.: 44-1-340-5715.
- Hargrove Entertainment, Inc., 139-18 84th Drive No.10, Briarwood, NY 11435-1855, U.S.A., tel.: 718-657-0542.

▶ *Figure 7*   *(continued)*

Individuals and Small Business Nontheatrical (Documentary and Educational) Distribution

Independent producers use many methods for documentary and educational program distribution. Here we mention three possible avenues. The story of how one producer achieved success illustrates the many ingredients in successful marketing for the independent producer.

Some people rely on independent distribution agencies. For example, one individual has a little company that makes films for unions on issues of education, safety, and union history. He distributes directly through the United Auto Workers and the Chemical Workers. Other individual independents are affiliated with a cooperative distribution agency for small documentary producers called New Day Films (22 River View Drive, Wayne, NJ 07470-3191. Tel: 201-633-0212), a collaborative whose members share expenses. New Day films had one film on male sexuality based on a weekend discussion group, another on a men's group of former wife beaters who were trying to break their past behavior. The potential audiences were small and specialized.[9]

Other independent producers and co-producers may work through specialized

distributors and festivals including those mentioned in the preceding section (see Figure 7). The market and festival circuit provides an excellent way to get exposure for one's production. Contacts can be made that result in a co-production through a presale. In addition to the outlets listed in Figure 7, small businesses and independent documentary produces should note the following markets and festivals:

- Sunny Side of the Doc, 3 Square Stalingrad, 13001 Marseilles, France, tel.: 33-91-08-43-15; fax: 33-91-84-38-34. This annual international festival is just for documentaries.
- Documentary Film Festival of New York, 454 Broome St., New York, NY, 10013, U.S.A., tel.: 212-966-9578. This annual event focuses on emerging film- and videomakers.
- The National Educational Film Video Festival, 655 13th St., Oakland, CA 94612, U.S.A., tel.: 415-465-6885.

Some independent producers are discovering video publishing. The process of marketing cassettes and bypassing broadcast video was discussed earlier in this chapter. Such tapes might be published to accompany the sale of a book, to provide "how to" material to supplement a manual, or to offer more realistic travel planning.

Bob Michelson's experience is a further illustration of the successful marketing of a documentary by an independent producer. Graduating from high school in 1974, he began to earn a living taking wedding photos and videos. By 1983 he had his own business. By 1991 his half-hour documentary, "Return from the Sea: The Restoration of Atlantic Salmon to New England," was shown on seven out of eight PBS stations in the northeastern United States, and he had signed an agreement to co-produce a 13-part half-hour documentary series on endangered species. Michelson says that all someone needs to say to him is "it's never been done before, and you can't do it." He then moves mountains to do it.

"I was writing an article on salmon for a magazine. I do underwater videography and decided to try out my new Hi-8 underwater video system to shoot some tape. The documentary was really an afterthought.

"The Hi-8 was fantastic. We bumped it up to beta and did our subcutting on beta, matched it off-line on one inch, and had an excellent broadcast quality end product."[10] Michelson's friend Paul Norton, daytime program manager for a local cable system, spent his evenings and weekends writing the script and preparing the story boards.

"Once I got started," says Michelson, "I spent months researching—first the product, then the subject, then how best to sell it. Three months after it was complete it was sold to the PBS stations. I had taken nothing, made it into something, and got it sold. Prior to this, I had sold underwater videography footage to various broadcast houses, but I had never before had broadcast credits for a program that I owned and produced. I started with lists, refined the lists, made calls to find out what they wanted and who to contact. I sent out letters—carefully worded letters that wouldn't land in the wastebasket—with sample footage in story board form. I made follow-up calls.

"I tried national cable outlets and PBS, and everyone wanted a series—not one half-hour program. Someone at PBS suggested that the individual stations might be

interested. Once I had signed with the individual stations, the program was shown in six million homes in the northeastern United States and the Canadian maritime provinces.

"Now, I've placed the program with a distributor. But I didn't want to start that way. The drawback in dealing with a distributor is that you can wait a long time before you get any result."[11]

Michelson has a lot of advice for the independent producer. Critical to signing a distribution contract is the control of the rights. He encourages the producer to have a top-notch lawyer and to carefully investigate any distributor before signing. Find out what the distributor distributes, how well, and whether other clients are satisfied with the contractual relationship. "You're tying your own hands. You create a product; then you give it to someone else whom you don't even know—maybe for five years. Maintain some control. I maintain ownership of my stock rights; I can repackage the material in another format any time. When I sold stock footage I sold only one time rights; if the program in which my footage appears is syndicated, I get paid."[12]

Michelson acknowledges that being in the right place at the right time, with the right capability and the right subject matter, was an important component of his success. But he reminds others that success depends also on finding something you really enjoy and doing what you do better than anyone else. "Everybody else thinks success will come from copying somebody else; find your own niche."[13]

One thing leads to another. His success with the salmon documentary has led him to sign for a co-production of a thirteen-part half-hour series on endangered species. His co-producer will cover many of field costs and post-production costs, and he'll do the creative work. In the end, he'll co-own something that could never have been produced if he'd had to cover some $300,000 in costs by himself.

Institutional News Distribution

In news distribution, too, the method of distribution depends upon whether one works for a network, a local station, or a large institution or whether one is an independent producer, either on contract with a large institution or working free-lance. The patterns are similar whether one is a single producer or a co-producer dealing with news. The principle difference is that timing is the essential ingredient in news coverage. One can't take time to negotiate co-production arrangements between the coverage of the story and the distribution. Prior understandings are required.

The assumption made in looking at the first model below is that the individual producer (or co-production partnership) either works for, or is on contract to, a station or network through which international distribution occurs. The European Broadcasting Union (EBU) model, while limited in distribution to member stations, is useful in that it illustrates one type of news distribution and, especially, because Pierre Brunel-Lantenac's descriptions acquaint the reader with aspects of news distribution that are even more important than the mechanics.

Lantenac compares news distribution during two middle east wars—two decades apart. In doing so, he vividly describes the changes technology has brought to the world of news distribution.

"In August 1990 it became clear that we must cover this growing crisis in the

Persian Gulf. My two superiors and the 37 stations who belong to the EBU—also my bosses—made this policy decision. Individual stations send crews, sound staff, satellite news gathering (SNG) equipment, whatever to the Persian Gulf. EBU's job is to help them to repatriate their picture in the most efficient and least expensive way."[14]

By early 1991, during Operation Desert Storm, EBU's setup was complex. In Israel, it had two airplanes—that is, two ways out of Jerusalem. It also had a crew coordinating all the satellite transmissions.

In Jordan, EBU had a permanent uplink in Amman. Part of the problem there was that for the correspondents to travel from the hotels and embassies to the television studios they had to cross a Palestinian area. Lantenac notes, "this was very dangerous because of the war tensions. A car was destroyed. Someone was attacked with a knife. So we established a portable ground link from the Intercontinental Hotel roof (where all journalists stay) to the earth station and then from there to the satellite. We have two coordinators on site in Amman.[15]

In Saudi Arabia, EBU had an uplink with two coordinators and some very light equipment for production. In addition, the EBU had a second transportable uplink, ready on wheels with a large camper with its own generators and two four-wheel trucks ready to follow the front when the ground battle started. The coalition troops had the mission of retaking Kuwait City from the Iraqis who had invaded Kuwait. EBU's objective was to support the journalists who would arrive just after the first troops to cover the liberation and to be witness to what was happening there. "To make possible such instant global distribution of the news from the mobile units going into Kuwait, it was necessary to meet with the Emir to receive clearance for this. That's the protocol in every country. But approving the mobile unit under these circumstances was not as simple as approving an uplink," Lantenac remembers.

"The logistics of providing this coverage includes far more than staffing the points for transmission. In a war one must pay a large license fee to each national government in order to operate in that country. We paid $45,000 per week in Jordan, $100,000 per month in Saudi Arabia, and similar amounts in other countries. All this money must come from the annual fees paid by our EBU member stations. We must also finance the transporting of all our technical equipment and personnel. During early 1991, it was necessary to charter three planes in one four-week period. I'm proud because twice I've succeeded in obtaining clearance for a civilian plane to land in Dahrain, Saudi Arabia, at a U.S. military base. I can't exaggerate the difficulty. Just for Dahrain since the beginning of the crisis, we have spent 6,000,000 Swiss francs plus 6,200,000 Swiss francs, plus 600,000 U.S. dollars to cover our transportation costs, the per diem for our engineers, technicians, and journalists, to arrange the uplink, and to pay all the fees. But it's important to do this because, without this organization, it would be practically impossible for news stations in a large part of the world to receive pictures from the war.

"My ladies and men—the women are very active in this crisis, that's a first in international war coverage—I hate it, but I find more female than male volunteers. I don't know why. Maybe it is this new generation. There's a young girl, just twenty-nine, behind the war front. Others too.

"My girls and my boys are not dealing with any kind of journalistic decision.

They receive the journalist's cassette and handle the live transmission of it. We did respect the censorship requests, however. A war is a war. As a newsman, I hate censorship. Armies must understand the need of a newsperson to do his/her job. But during a war, a newsperson must respect that his/her scoop might give information to the other side. It's a problem. Most of the people doing this job in the Persian Gulf crisis are now, for the first time, war correspondents. They are courageous. Sometimes they don't understand that a war is a war."[16]

Commenting on wartime censorship in the distribution of news, Lantenac observed that technology is, in large part, responsible for the change in the rules. He believes that the turning point on war news coverage came with the Falkland War in 1981, when Argentina tried to regain the Falkland Islands from England. Technology delivered the news a bit too quickly. The British Army invoked an embargo and censorship to protect its operations. The real pictures came at the end of the war. Then ITN did a documentary. "War coverage showing coffins and jungle battles as was done in the Vietnam War is gone," Lantenac notes. "Today we have TV war news coverage without pictures that show the devastation of war. CNN's Persian Gulf War coverage is the best example. Its coverage was of the correspondents. For me it's a little too much like Hollywood."[17]

Technology can distribute the information much more rapidly in the 1990s than in the 1960s and 1970s. Military leaders have learned to oppose the transmission of pictures that they feel might damage their effort. Two things happen: the enemy might see things that compromise military strategy, and the public might decide that war is nasty stuff—as happened eventually with the American public's opposition to keeping U.S. troops in Vietnam.

"But," Lantenac comments, "the most striking difference between now and former wars is the matter of distribution. I covered the 1967 Six Day War, when Israel preempted an attack planned by Egypt, Jordan, and Syria. We had no satellite. We had no video. We'd shoot our film. Seal the film box. Give the box to a cab driver. The driver would rush it to the coast. There we'd charter a small boat to Cyprus. In Cyprus, a motor bike driver would speed from the harbor to the air base. The film would be put on a plane to Rome. In Rome, another motor bike drive would rush the box to a studio. Then to Eurovision network. This was not so long ago."[18]

Independent News Distribution

One of the best opportunities for independent producers in news is to provide a news co-production as a *video news release* (VNR).

A producer or co-producers should find a corporation or institution to pay for the production of a video news release. There are many reasons why an institution might want to do this. For example, a national magazine might offer news directors an interview with a controversial personality (*Playboy* offered interviews with Jessica Hahn, the subject of the TV evangelist sex scandal.) A special event promotes a national charity fund-raising, and the charity might find televising the event helpful to national fund-raising. For example, NFL football players gathered in Central Park for a game of touch football on behalf of a charity. A government agency might want

a news story distributed that otherwise might not be covered. For example, the U.S. Treasury Secretary issues a statement on tax reform and the gold standard—an item of interest to a select audience only. Political candidates and elected officials may want to convey a message to their constituency. For example, for the first time, in 1988, most of the U.S. presidential candidates used satellite technology to make possible transmission of local debates, to address specialized audiences of college students, and to be interviewed by local newsroom reporters.)[19]

The independent producer/co-producer negotiates a contract that includes (1) remuneration for production costs for a piece approximately 90 seconds long, including any desired computer graphics, (2) fees for the selected distribution services, (3) a producer remuneration percentage for each of the number of places to which the production was distributed.

Medialink in New York was the first integrated system dedicated to the distribution of video new releases. This service started in the late 1980s as a follow-up to other services initiated in 1986 to service the networks and stations that were being inundated with a multiplicity of satellite downlinks, modems, fax machines, telephones, and mail. There was too much information to deal with in the time available. Medialink's newswire was created to highlight and synthesize what was being received. Westinghouse, CNN, INN, and Conus send urgent news advisories on the news wire.[20]

The principle problem for the producer and the sponsoring organization is to distinguish between a news story and a promotional commercial. The first stands a good chance of being well received by stations to which it is distributed. The second can be irritating. Beyond that, the greater the likelihood that the VNR is 'hard news' the greater the likelihood that it will be shown. Timing is critical. Local interest is critical. However, some documentary or background pieces are used when appropriate occasions arise.

A distribution company like Medialink will make available a wide range of distribution choices for the producer and the client. One can transmit the VNR via satellite or mail cassettes. One can accompany the transmission with various kinds of prenotification—by satellite, by telephone, or by mail. One can contract for various methods of monitoring results—television "clipping" service, telephone polls, and before long, an invisible electronic code, called Sigma, implanted in each specific VNR.

New technology opens new doors for the independent producer wanting to embark upon distributing news stories. It just takes a lot of producer initiative.

Institutional Drama and Entertainment Distribution

Grenada Television provides a good example of co-production distribution in entertainment television. As discussed previously, Grenada created a new section focused on entertainment films for television. Grenada Executive Vice President Dighton Spooner describes how he acquires programs. "I initiate the projects. I have staff and a new department. U.S. and European producers submit proposals to me and we assess those. Ideas are registered. I have an assistant who works with me to identify projects. We also have readers who help with that. In addition, we also look

for books from which we can develop scripts for programs. And we also generate original program ideas ourselves.[21]

West Deutsche Rundfunk (WDR) has a similar approach. "We have a department that does buying and selling software, and this department is also responsible for generating co-productions. If they find someone in France or somewhere with an interesting project, they then look here at WDR for a journalist who likes the idea and wants to see the production happen. A match is made," says WDR's Manfred Jenke.[22]

The festivals provide a place for entertainment co-production matchmaking. Production and distribution deals result. For example, at the 1991 MIPCOM festival Asian partners began to emerge in co-production deals. A 26-part half-hour documentary/entertainment series called "Spies" will be produced by CBS, Tokyo Broadcasting System, Arts & Entertainment, and video mail order club Columbia House. CBS will have worldwide television distribution rights outside Japan. A&E has U.S. cable rights. Columbia has the video and other rights. Also at the 1991 MIPCOM, a Korean network, MBC, is co-producing with Saban International and French Broadcaster TFI a children's animated series "Around the World in Eighty Dreams."[23]

Syndication, of course, is the principal mode of distribution for broadcast entertainment television. The U.S. Federal Communications Commission defines syndication (47 CFR 76.5p) as "any program sold, licensed, or distributed or offered to television stations in more than one market within the United States for noninterconnected television broadcast exhibitions, but not including live presentation." In other words, the buyer is licensed to use the product for a limited period. For the co-producer, syndication becomes an option through the contract process with a buyer who accepts the program for broadcast.

Individual and Small Business Drama Distribution

Susan Ryan, independent distribution consultant, describes the special niche allocated for individual and small business drama distribution, "I started in distribution with independents in the late 70s. At that time the independents were getting much more recognition in Europe than in the U.S. At festivals in Europe many independent filmmakers were able to get funding from sources there for co-productions. For example, England's Channel 4 was an exciting new outlet for independents and especially for those producing culturally diverse programming. In the early 80s there wasn't an independent filmmaker in the United States that wasn't sending requests to Channel 4 because they seemed to have quite a vast amount of resources and a lot of programming time." Channel 4 has funded many of these artists. In addition, they have engaged in aggressive global searches for talented third-world producers. In the late 80s that changed somewhat. Less money was available. Less air time was available. But Channel 4 remains a jewel in the crown of opportunity for innovative production.

Ryan notes, when it comes to theatrical distribution, the marketplace is constantly changing. It's hard to say whom to contact, how to proceed. As soon as a plan seems evident, the situation will have changed again. "A person might start with

Independent Feature Project (IFP) [see Chapter 6]. There's a place called Off Hollywood that focuses on American independent films for a specialized market. It does case studies of very big independent films like 'Good Fight' 'El Norte,' etc. An organization like IFP will tell you which distributors are looking for which type film."

The Independent Feature Project in New York assists independent filmmakers in the United States. Every year it has a market where it brings in foreign buyers and potential co-producers. It screens rough cuts of films, helps people get added funding, and shows sample reels that people might use as co-productions.

"Get your co-production into the New York Film Festival and others such as those in Chicago, Seattle, and San Francisco," says Ryan. "Get exposure. For video, participate in educational festivals—things like the American Film Festival. Also, participate in the National Educational Film Festival in Oakland. [See Figure 8 for entertainment festival and marketplace addresses.] I've mentioned only two major festivals. Again, there are many others."[24]

To prepare yourself for submitting your work to a potential distributor or as a festival entry, it's important to know what some might consider the criteria for success. Then you can measure your production against those criteria to evaluate whether or not you think it is likely to sell.

Susan Ryan comments on criteria she has seen people use: "There are films you fall in love with. That's an initial emotional reaction. Also, you know there are markets for a certain kinds of films—for example, those that deal with women's issues have a certain audience. If it's had some festival exposure, you can see how well it's been received. But it's always a gamble. The successful production is often something that has a different theme or approach—something where there's not been a whole lot else done. Check to see what's already out there. I would lean toward an interesting and well made film despite the fact that it might not have the largest fad appeal."[25]

Just as producers worry about cost, so must distributors. There's a difference dealing with independent producers and dealing with an institution like a broadcast station. A big institution might have the negative and be able to easily supply some prints. Working with a small entity or an independent producer is risky for small distributors. Susan Ryan observes, "Small distributors want to hook up with a producer that has some materials so it's not necessary to invest a lot of money in having a negative made or a one inch master. Independents don't always come with something to distribute. There are lots of questions, and a lot of costs. For example, who pays for the subtitles? Do you subtitle the negative or just engrave on two or three prints if that's all you think will sell?"[26]

Another avenue open to the independent co-producer is to advertise in magazines like *The Telco Report* (see Chapter 6). This magazine describes itself as "the only weekly publication of international television programming." It highlights the major industry markets and festivals and regularly carries paragraph-long descriptions of many types of programs available for distribution—documentaries and news as well as entertainment and drama. The productions listed are offered by large institutions, distributors, and independents. For example, Radio Netherlands

Television in Hilversum, Holland, offered a series of ten 8–14 minute documentary productions on Netherlands handicrafts, ranging from diamond cutting to wooden shoe making; CS Associates in Mill Valley, California, offered 22 minutes of entertainment in "No Easy Way Out"; Riverside Aps in Copenhagen offered a 12 minute animated humorous film for adults called "Solo"; Alliance International of Montreal offered a 90 minute entertainment production called "Coming of Age"; ZDF in Mainz, Germany, offers video news magazines including one called "USA: The Selling of a Hero—Schwarzkopf."[27]

Entertainment Festivals and Markets

Markets and festivals, discussed briefly in regard to documentaries, are a major forum for buying and selling drama and entertainment programs. Aside from MIP,

---

- MIPCOM is the second largest international festival. It is held in the fall in the Mediterranean mecca of Cannes on Cote d'Azur, France. (MIPCOM, Palais des Festivals, Cannes, France.) Over 7500 TV, Cable, Video or Satellite industry professionals from 80 countries attended the 1991 market.
- The International TV Film Festival of Monte Carlo was founded in 1961 by Prince Ranier of Monaco to review the world's best television productions in a competition of television and video. (International Television Festival of Monte Carlo, Concentration Centre, C Cam Blvd., Louise II, 98000 Monte Carlo, Monaco, tel.: 33-93-304-944.) At this annual winter event, each exhibiting company has its own private screening room.
- The Berlin International Film Festival holds an annual competition. Contact: Berlin International Film Festival, Budapesterstrasse 50, 1000 Berlin, 30 Germany, tel.: 49-30-254-890; fax: 49-30-254-89-249.
- Edinburgh International Film Festival, Filmhouse, 88 Lothian Road, Edinburgh EH 9BZ, Scotland, tel.: 31-288-4051; fax: 31-229-5501.
- International Film and Television Festival of New York, 655 Avenue of the Americas, Second Floor, New York, NY, 10010, U.S.A., tel.: 914-238-4481; fax: 914-238-5040.
- Montreal World Film Festival, 1455 De Maisonneuve Blvd., W., Suite H 109, Montreal PQ H3G 1M8, Quebec, Canada, tel.: 514-848-3883; fax: 514-848-3886.
- The American Film Market Association comprises 74 companies distributing, marketing, and in many cases, producing feature motion pictures—only secondarily for television. It sponsors the American Film Market.
- Banff Television Festival is an annual event first launched in 1979. Its emphasis is the the co-production marketplace for television professionals wanting to meet, exchange and develop ideas, and initiate projects. It takes only made-for-television entries in a wide range of areas.

▶ *Figure 8   Some Entertainment Festivals and Markets.* (*Source:* Television International, *Vol. 32, No. 5 [Fall/Spring 1989–1990]. Television International Publications, P.O. Box 2430, Hollywood, CA 90028, tel.: 818-795-8386; fax: 818-795-8436.*)

mentioned in the discussion about "Nova," there are many other festivals and marketplaces. Some examples are listed in Figure 8.

The options for distribution of your co-productions are considerable. The hardest part is getting started—getting people to pay attention to your work amidst the clatter of thousands of other distractions. A quality product, a clever approach, some money, a lot of persistence, and being in the right place at the right time—these are the ingredients that can make the difference in reaching your distribution objectives. These ingredients need not be added in any specific order or amounts. Remember the person who got the production funding because she already had the distribution agreement. But especially remember that anything *is* possible.

Notes

1. Personal interview with Susan Ryan, Independent Distribution Consultant, 3285 33rd St., #B1, Astoria, NY 11106, August 22, 1991.
2. Personal interview with Lydia Stephans, Director, Programming, ABC Sports, 47 West 66th Street, New York, NY 10023, tel.: 212-456-3702, August 23, 1991.
3. Ryan interview.
4. Personal interview with Alain Jehlan, Director of Acquisitions, "Nova," WGBH, Boston, August 27, 1991.
5. Ibid.
6. Personal interview with Richard Sydenham, Producer, Special Programs Section, Department of Information, United Nations, Room S-955, New York, NY 10017, Fax: 212-963-4556, tel.: 212-963-6944.
7. Ibid.
8. U.N. advertisement directing reader to the Director of the Information Products Division, Mr. Georges Leclere, Room S-837 A, U.N. Audio Visual Promotion and Distribution Unit, New York, NY 10017, fax: 212-963-0765. *Telco Report,* Telco Productions, 2730 Wilshire Blvd., Suite 404, Santa Monica, CA 90403, Vol. 23, No. 24, July 22, 1991.
9. Jehlan interview.
10. Telephone interview with Bob Michelson, Photos by Michelson, Inc.,P.O. Box 93, Braintree, MA 02184, tel.: 617-848-8870, October 21, 1991.
11. Ibid.
12. Ibid.
13. Ibid.
14. Personal interview with Pierre Brunel-Lantenac, Director, News Operations, European Broadcasting Union, Ancienne Route 17a/Casa Postale 67, CH-1218 Grand Saconnex, Geneva, Switzerland, Fax: 022-798-5897, tel.: 022-717-2821, February 22, 1991.
15. Ibid
16. Ibid.
17. Ibid.
18. Ibid.
19. *The TV News Release Handbook* (Medialink, Video News Service, 708 3rd Avenue, New York, NY 10017, tel.: 800-843-0677, fax: 212-682-2370), 1990. Examples sighted were Medialink clients.

20. Ibid.

21. Personal interview with Dighton E. Spooner, Jr., Executive Vice President, Films for Television, Grenada Television, 36 Golden Square, London W1R 4AH, England, fax: 213-282-8992, tel.: 213-282-8996, February 15, 1991.

22. Personal interview with Dr. Manfred Jenke, Director of Broadcasting, Westdeutscher Rundfunk, Appellhofplatz 1, Postfach 10 19 50, 5000 Koln, Germany, fax: 49-221-220-3539, tel.: 49-221-220-4140, February 27, 1991.

23. "Co-productions, Animation, Top MIPCOM Activity," Broadcasting (Cahners, 1705 DeSales Street, Washington, DC, 20035, October 14, 1991), p. 23.

24. Ryan interview.

25. Ibid.

26. Ibid.

27. *The Telco Report* (Telco Productions, 2730 Wilshire Blvd., Suite 404, Santa Monica, CA 90403, tel.: 213-828-4003, fax: 213-828-3340), Vol. 23, No. 22 and No. 24, July 1, 1991 and July 15, 1991.

6

▼
▼
▼
▼
▼

Opportunities, Contacts, and Resource Lists

CAREERS IN INTERNATIONAL CO-PRODUCTION

Focus

One of the best ways to provide insight on how best to succeed in a new career is to look both at the advice and at the example set forth by professionals now working in that field. Dighton Spooner, Vice President of Granada Television, has strong words of advice for the person interested in international co-production. "What should one tell a newcomer to this field? Tell them that deals do not make programs. You can have all the elaborate relationships you want between companies, but you need sound ideas. Compelling stories and stories that galvanize people make these relationships work. You can have a nice structure, but it's the programs that are the most important thing.

"I think that it's important to remember, when working with a group of people, that a creative vision and a creative point of view are critical for audience satisfaction, because, ultimately, the audience has to make an emotional connection with the characters in a story. This means that to produce a successful product, the final responsibility for the creative decisions must be specifically allocated. If you have too many cooks, it will be no one's vision. And clear vision makes good story telling work.

"Don't say I decided to go into co-production. Say I decided to go into the business of making television programs. If you shifted into another business—say, making cars—you wouldn't necessarily start with how to get a bank loan. You'd start with a creative vision of what you want the car to look like and why someone would want to buy it. Similarly, co-production is simply a mechanism that allows you to bring something creative to fruition."[1]

The advice offered by a professional in educational video is similar to that of Spooner. Jim Stevenson, Executive Director of the Educational Broadcasting Services Trust, observes that the newcomers he's worked with both at the BBC and at EBS "think the world begins and ends with a toy. I try to tell them there's more out there. When I first joined the BBC, my boss said that for the first two years I would be fascinated with technique. Later I would begin to assume the technique and begin to get on with the real business of thinking about what people needed. Especially

now, with the rapid changes in technologies, people become entranced by technique. It's shortsighted."[2]

Preparation

Leonid A. Zolotarevsky, Director of the Department for International Programming, U.S.S.R. National State Broadcasting System (Gosteleradio) and Director of Sovtelexport, has worked on many international co-productions in recent years. He observes that, "to do co-production, a person must know what television is like in the other countries with which you collaborate, to know about the social and political background of the people in those countries, to know what their financial background is. This kind of job demands a lot of expertise and a lot of knowledge. And of course, you'll be most successful if you know a foreign language—for us, and for many people throughout the world, it's best to know English.

"Then, of course, a person should be a professional in television journalism. It involves not only journalism but some knowledge of the roles of directors, camera operators, and producers. The person should be well acquainted with the finances and the logistics of television and how television differs from one country to another. For example, Russian television is not very much like American television. It's entirely different in programming, in financing, in sponsorship. French television has nothing to do with either the U.S. or Russia.

"One doesn't need to have been a veteran of television for a long time. Young people on my staff can get acquainted with their aspect of the work in just three or four months, but they have a very good educational background. By that I mean that they have a knowledge of world culture, literature, journalism, and foreign language. With all that preparation, a young person could enter the business in just a few months."[3]

Dighton Spooner similarly urges a solid educational background. His emphasis complements Zolotarevsky's. "I advise people not to take courses in television production. I advise people to have a passion for something—music, dance, science, theater, literature. Have something to say. It's more important to have a desire to say something than to think you know about the process. In fact, we can teach someone the mechanics of how to edit, how to work with a crew—but, we can't teach them how to write, we can't teach them how to think. We can't teach them to know an area like business, arts, or politics. So learn about something that can be the subject matter—the basis for your professional career—then marry that with the process. I majored in politics. I also consider television a journeyman's profession in that it has an apprentice system where you learn one job, master it, and move up."[4]

Lydia Stephans from ABC sports reminds the reader that there are many ways to find a career niche. "All students want to be an on air reporter. They have no idea what happens behind the scenes. I wish the schools paid more attention to what happens behind the scenes, because that is really the way to get involved in TV. If you want to be on air, get a journalism degree, take speech classes, look right, dress properly. Some people are not cut out for that. Emphasizing looks and speech discourages them. There's a wealth of opportunity behind the scenes in television production and co-production. For example, you could start out in PR helping to promote what will be on TV, or start in journalism by writing for people who will be

on TV or write scripts for soap operas. There are communication spots where you are interacting with people in all facets of the profession. There are technical needs. Engineers must set up cameras, wire the studio, cable the truck. There are camera person positions for people with a photography background and a sense of creativity. There are audio jobs. There are the wonderful voices in the promos—they make about $300,000 per year. They're lucky. They sit home until they get a call to read a promo. Norman Rose has the most wonderful voice in world. You've heard him on commercials and on ABC sports. But no one knows what he looks like. There's jobs for people with a business degree in rights and acquisitions—like my job. For that you need good communication and business skills.

"The international fields are wide open. Be bilingual. Have some communications background—not necessarily a degree. Intern in a station and decide your area of focus. The international field is diverse and growing rapidly—read a lot of newspapers and magazines to keep up with new changes in the business. For example, read *Electronic Media,* and *Variety.*"[5]

For those interested in surviving in hard economic times, the advice from Tony Goodman, Deputy Director of the International Visual Communications Association (IVCA), is directed toward those interested in professions in corporate video. But it might be equally useful advise for persons in any aspect of television production. "Learn to specialize in something like technical video, medical video, financial services video, or whatever subset of your field is the area that interests you and might also have economic promise in the next few years."[6]

Finally, a bit of practical advice for the person choosing independent co-production. Alain Jehlan from PBS's "Nova" series comments, "If you start out as independent, you have the freedom to define your topic of interest, but your trade-off is that you must spend a disproportionate amount of your time hustling for funds. The alternative is to compromise and work within a larger institution, hopefully placed in a spot that suits your interests and talents."[7]

Choosing the Right Jobs

If you are launching a career, the entire road map is ahead of you. There may be alternative roads leading to the same destination, not just one turnpike. It's interesting to note the varied routes taken by some of the people who are prominent in their field.

Dighton Spooner is now a successful Executive Vice President of Films for Television, Granada Television, London. He began his career as a kid from an urban minority neighborhood in Cambridge, Massachusetts. Interested in photography, he started working when he was 17, using his still photos as a way to get a job as a studio cameraman. At Northeastern University he took courses in film history—because he liked film, not because he saw it as an avenue to a career. He also studied pharmacology, Chinese foreign policy, civil liberties, and art history. He sees this diversity as extremely helpful to his present job.

He worked for WGBH, the public television station in Boston, focusing on arts, music, and children's and dramatic programming. Then he went to Los Angeles and received offers from CBS and HBO. He took a CBS job in its miniseries department and stayed 3 years before he met his current boss when they were both on a panel

about a co-production at the Edinburgh Festival. The conversations that day resulted in his being hired by Grenada in London.[8]

Susan Ryan, independent distribution consultant, never expected to work in distribution. But once involved, she found it was the perfect combination of her love for film and her background in economics. Besides, she didn't like producing films. She liked to watch films. Before she moved to New York, she had worked in a movie theater and knew what a box office report was. In New York, she started as a volunteer at the Independent Feature Project while it was organizing an annual conference. There she learned about a job in a new distribution company. "The company started with two employees, four films, a board of filmmakers, and an incredibly dynamic older woman named Fran Spielman. She was helping this new company pioneer in the idea of distributing independent documentaries to theatrical audiences. Not a lot of people did that. That was 1978. We'd watch a lot of films—look at the processing, work out the acquisition, talk with people about film, convince people that the films will make some money, perhaps not a lot of money. I watched the company grow from two to six and from four films to fifty or sixty films."[9]

Later Ryan moved more into educational distribution. There, writing skills mattered. She wrote brochures, study guides, and catalogues and worked with filmmakers.

Independent video producer, filmmaker, and author Herb Fuller commented on how independents get jobs. "Get exposure through competition presentations. Grease the old boys' network. Look in video stores—rent travel videos, see who makes them. Hook up with entry level jobs for travel video companies—they don't pay well, but they give you a track record. If you speak an uncommon language, go to that country and identify the American presence and determine how you can be useful to such institutions or businesses because you are American and also bilingual. Check the embassy—especially the commercial attaché. Embassies are not only for extradition. They exist to help international ventures. Work for free in public television, and perhaps a paying job will evolve because you are in the right place at the right time.

"For me, the potential clients for my job in Thailand looked at work I had done. They hired one company and one individual on a contract basis to produce the program with the appropriate people in Thailand. I was the individual. Other shoots worked much the same way."[10]

In order to secure any of the specific kinds of jobs discussed in the preceding paragraphs, one must keep one's sights focused on the overall job market—the global neighborhood. The person whose career will span into the 21st century cannot afford to limit her or his horizons to the neighboring town or state. The world has changed dramatically. Hear the words of CNN International Vice President Peter Vesey: "The future of any economy is now linked to the global economy, to the trends and the political ideas that are being interchanged between nations and groups of nations. To survive and compete well in this environment, a person's education and his or her perspective must be to look across oceans. Schools and universities have not yet caught up with the changes in the world; they do not yet aim people in the right career directions. The gold is no longer in the California hills. It may be in Chile or Japan or Indonesia, or other places most people can't even find on the map."[11]

CONTACTS

Earlier chapters of this book introduced you to contacts appropriate to the particular topics discussed at that time. The information here will be complementary—identifying organizations, markets, and publications useful to both the student and the new professional interested in international co-production.

Organizations
Association of Independent Video and Film Makers (AIVF)
625 Broadway, 9th Floor
New York, NY 10012
Tel.: 212-473-3400
AIVF is a clearinghouse with regional offices across the United States. It has done workshops on international co-production—funding, customs, shipping and distribution. It has a library in its office.

International Television Association (ITVA)
6311 North O'Connor Road, LB 51
Irving, TX 75039
Tel.: 214-869-1112
ITVA represents a wide range of institutional, educational, corporate, and interactive nonbroadcast TV producers in the United States and 14 other countries. It provides its 14,000 members with information and referral services to advance nonbroadcast communications. It holds an annual international video festival and convention.

International Association for Film and Video Communications (IVCA)
Bolsover House, 5/6 Clipstone Street
London W1P 7EB
Tel.: 44-71-580-0962
Fax: 44-71-436-2606
IVCA literature says it is the professional association for corporate visual communications. It sponsors a festival for business communications. The award categories include attitudinal and motivational training productions, practical training, corporate health and safety, education, recruitment, sales products, sales service, public display, corporate image, public relations, internal communications, regular employee communications, medical productions, public welfare and safety productions, video publishing, and interactive video.[12]

Independent Program Producers Association (IPPA)
50-51 Berwick St.
London, W1A - 41D
England
Tel.: 44-71-439-7034
Fax: 44-71-494-2700
In 1991, IPPA published a book called *Co-Production Europe*, edited by Janet Watson. The IPPA is the association for professionals interested in broadcast televi-

sion. One important listing in the IPPA book is the independent producers' list from Coordination Européenne des Producteurs Independants (CEPI). CEPI is the umbrella group founded to assist independent producers (see Figure 9).

AUSTRIA
F.A.F.O.
(Fachverband der Audiovisions und
Filmindustrie Osterriechs)
Wiedner Haupstrasse 63
P.O. Box 327, 1045 Wien
Tel: (1) 93 76 74
Fax: (1) 96 43 28
Contact: Michael von Wolkenstein

BELGIUM
U.P.P.T.
(Union Professionelle des Producteurs
de Programmes de Télévision)
21 rue Rasson
1040 Bruxelles
Tel: (2) 736 54 37
Fax: (2) 736 52 39
Contact: Pierre Levie

DENMARK
PRODUCENTERNE
(Association of Film, TV, Video & AV
Producers)
Vesterbrogade 37
1620 Copenhagen V
Tel: (31) 22 16 36
Fax: (31) 22 06 47
Contact: Ebbe Preisler

FEDERAL REPUBLIC
OF GERMANY
B.V.D.F.P.
(BundesverbandDeutscher Fernseh-
produzenten)
Widenmayerstrasse 32
8000 Mönchen 22
Tel: (89) 22 35 35
Fax: (89) 228 55 62
Contact: Claus Hardt

FRANCE
U.S.P.A.
(Union Syndicale de la Production
Audiovisuelle)
19 rue Réamur
75003 Paris
Tel: (1) 42 71 23 61
Fax: (1) 42 71 82 65
Contact: Alain Modot

GREECE
S.P.E.T.
(Association des Producteurs de la
Télévision Hellénique)
c/o Dionyssis Samiotis
39 Solonos Street
10672 Athens
Tel: (1) 36 47 878
Fax: (1) 36 01 328
Contact: George Sgourakis

ITALY
A.I.C.E.T.
(Associazione Imprenditori Cinema e
Televisione)
c/o Clesi Films
24 via F. Carrara
00196 Roma
Tel: (6) 361 37 71
Fax: (6) 361 08 54
Contact: Silvio Clementelli

THE NETHERLANDS
O.T.P.
(Vereniging van Onafhanelijke Televisie
Producenten)
Vaartweg 66
1217 SV Hilversum
Tel: (35) 218 241
Fax: (35) 218 984
Contact: Han Peekle

▶ *Figure 9*   *Resource Organizations for Coordination Européenne des Producteurs Inde-*
pendants (CEPI). (Source: Janet Watson, ed., 1990, Co-Production Europe, pp. 5–8, IPPA,
50–51 Berwick Street, London W1A 41D, tel.: 44-71-439-7034; fax: 44-71-494-42700.)

The National Association of Broadcasters (NAB)
1771 North Street NW
Washington, D.C. 20036
U.S.A.

Tel.: 202-429-5300

Fax: 202-429-5343

NAB hosts a 40,000 people trade show every year—one of best in industry. Lots of TV stations and equipment dealers belong. They also provide technical and legal information and have a research library.

Independent Feature Project

132 West 21st St.

New York, NY

Tel.: 212-243-7777

This group, with 1500 members assists independents and holds an annual American Independent Feature Film Market, involving film professionals, buyers, and agents. The market also includes seminars and workshops. IFP identifies potential funders for members and provides a library, a resource guide to distribution companies, a catalogue of scripts available for production, and computer referrals as appropriate. Its objective is to promote the production and distribution of feature films.

American Film and Video Association (AFVA)

8050 Milwaukee Avenue

P.O. Box 48659

Niles, IL 60648

Tel.: 708-698-6440.

An advocate for nontheatrical media, AFVA seeks funding, supports legislation and holds an annual festival for film, video and media. It has a library and data base to provide the producer with assistance and publishes both a quarterly journal and a bimonthly newsletter. The library can be reached by phone or fax daily to provide member assistance.

Society of Motion Picture Technicians and Engineers (SMPTE)

595 West Hartsdale Ave.

White Plains, NY 10607

Tel.: 914-761-1100

This group holds an annual conference in January/February. It publishes a list of technical terms translated into several languages. International expansion has been its priority since 1990. It now has branches in Germany, the former Soviet Union, Italy, Scandinavia, and New Zealand. Czechoslovakia, Hungary and Japan will likely join in the early 1990s. It sees its role in international standardization as particularly important.[13]

National Association of Television Program Executives (NAPTE)

10100 Santa Monica Blvd.

Suite 300

Los Angeles, CA 90067

Tel.: 213-282-8801

Fax: 213-282-0760

NAPTE holds an annual conference with workshops on advertising, promotion and syndication.

International Association of Independent Producers
P.O. Box 2801
Washington, DC 20013
Tel.: 202-775-1113
This organization of some 3400 members provides assistance and referral to members on such items as equipment exchange, personnel, sponsorship ideas, and scholarships. It also sponsors seminars in Europe, Asia, and Latin America.

Special Interest Video Association (SIVA)
P.O. Box 402
Oak Ridge, NJ 07438
Tel.: 201-697-7776
Fax: 201-697-5239
This group holds an annual convention. Its members include large and small production companies engaged in special interest production.

International Documentary Association
1551 South Robertson Blvd.
Los Angeles, CA 90035
Tel.: 213-284-8422
This group's mission is to promote nonfiction film and video throughout the world.

International Animated Film Association (IAFS)
5301 Laurel Canyon Blvd.
Suite 250
North Hollywood, CA 91607
Tel.: 818-508-5224
This group provides referrals, information, and some scholarships.

United States Information Service
1776 Pennsylvania Avenue NW
Washington, DC 20547
This U.S. government agency provides tapes and films to the U.S. State Department network of libraries and resource centers throughout the world.

International Teleconferencing Association
1299 Woodside Drive
McLean, VA 22102
Tel.: 703-556-6115

Western Union Teleconferencing, Inc.
105 G Street NW
Suite 200
Washington, DC 20005
Tel.: 202-624-0295
Telex: 892708
Since the early 1980s, these organizations have been staging, networking and

equipping video conferences using the Western Union–owned satellites and transmitting/receiving facilities.

VSN Satellite Communication Services
5 Crow Canyon Court
Suite 209
San Ramon, CA 94583
Tel.: 415-820-5563
This organization publishes *Teleconference Magazine*.

American CDI Association
11111 Santa Monica Boulevard
Suite 750
Los Angeles, CA 90025
Tel.: 213-444-6619
This association offers a producer's handbook and technical information.

International Teleproduction Society, Inc.
990 Avenue of the Americas
Suite 21 E
New York, NY 10018
This is the TV facilities trade association.

Sovtelexport
12 Karolyov St.
Moscow,
U.S.S.R.
Tel.: 7-095-217-9042
Fax: 7-095-288-9510
This is the new independent arm of Russian TV interested in co-productions.

Visnews
Visnews House
Cumberland Avenue
London NW10 7EH
England
Tel.: London: 44-81-965-7733
New York: 212-698-4500
This organization can provide camera crews and services worldwide.

Worldwide Television News (WTN)
The Interchange
Oval Road
Camden Lock
London, NW1
United Kingdom
Tel.: 44-071-410-5200
Fax: 44-071-413-8302
or

WTN
1705 De Sales Street N. W.
Washington, DC 20026
U.S.A.
Tel.: 202-887-7889
Fax: 202-887-7978
This organization can provide camera crews and services worldwide.

Third World Newsreel
335 West 38th St. 5th Floor
New York, NY.10018
Tel.: 212-947-9277
This alternative media organization is committed to the creation and appreciation of media by people of color in the United States and in developing communities throughout the world. They assist in film and video production training, distribution, and fiscal sponsorship.

National Black Programming Consortium
929 Harrison Avenue, Suite 104
Columbus, OH 43215
Tel.: 614-299-5355
This organization is a prominent resource center for Black producers.

The European Co-Production Association
c/o ZDF
Essenheimerstrasse
P.O. Box 4040
D-6500
Mainz, Germany
Tel.: 49-6131-705168
Fax: 49-6131-78060
This consortium of seven European public service television networks was established in 1985. Its members are from Italy, Switzerland, Germany, Spain, France, the United Kingdom, and Austria.

The European Economic Community has a range of pilot projects discussed in Chapter 3. The list of Economic Community coordinators for each of these projects is shown in Figure 10.

Small companies are always popping up and fading out. Sometimes associations also come and go. It would be wise to contact the public library or university libraries in a major city to examine media catalogues published by distribution firms and to check association directories as well as foundation resources and the periodicals mentioned in the publications section at the end of this chapter..

Another source of organizations interested in assisting in video production is government. Depending on where you are and what you want to do, you will need to identify the appropriate government office. For example, some jurisdictions incorporate video into their economic or tourism development programs. States may offer incentives to produce feature films or videos in their state. Remember the Tourism Board that assisted in the production in Madeira, Portugal. Others have agencies

Pilot Projects / Expériences Pilotes

PROJECTS / PROJETS	COORDINATORS / COORDINATEURS	
I.DISTRIBUTION		
European Film Distribution Office - **EFDO**	Mr. Dieter KOSSLICK Europäisches Filmbüro Friedensallee, 14-16 – D-2000 HAMBURG 50	TEL.: (40) 390.90.25 TLX: 216.53.55 EFDO-D FAX: (40) 390.62.49
Espace Vidéo Européen – **EVE**	Mr. David KAVANAGH Irish Film Institute Eustace Street, 6 – IRL - DUBLIN 2	TEL.: (1) 679.57.44 FAX: (1) 679.96.57
	M. Jean-Marie BEAULOYE Médiathèque de la Communauté Française de Belgique a.s.b.l. Place Flagey, 18 – B-1050 BRUXELLES	TEL.: (2) 640.38.15 FAX: (2) 640.02.91
Organisation Européenne pour un Marché de l'Audiovisuel Indépendant – **EURO AIM**	M. Rudi BARNET Rue des Minimes, 26 B-1000 BRUXELLES	TEL.: (2) 518.14.60 TLX: 64.917 RELINT-B FAX: (2) 512.86.57
Broadcasting Accross the Barriers of European Language – **BABEL**	M. Frank NAEF UER / EBU Case Postale, 67 CH-1218 GRAND-SACONNEX GENEVE	TEL.: (22) 717.21.11 TLX.: 41.57.00 EBU CH FAX: (22) 798.58.97
II. PRODUCTION		
Club d'Investissement **MEDIA**	M. Pierre MUSSO Institut National de la Communication Audiovisuelle (I.N.A.) Avenue de l'Europe, 4 F-94366 BRY-SUR-MARNE (PARIS)	TEL.: (1) 49.83.23.22 TLX: 23.11.94 INADIR FAX: (1) 49.83.25.82
European **SCRIPT** Fund	Mrs. Renee GODDARD Highbury Place, 39 C UK-LONDON N5 1QP	TEL.: (71) 226.99.03 FAX: (71) 354.27.06
CARTOON	M. Marc VANDEWEYER Mme Corinne JENART Rue Franz Merjay, 127 B-1060 BRUXELLES	TEL.: (2) 347.28.70 FAX: (2) 347.23.47
MAP-TV	M. Jean CHERASSE Avenue de l'Europe, 4 F-94366 BRY-SUR-MARNE (PARIS)	TEL.: (1) 49.83.27.45 FAX: (1) 49.83.25.84
III.FORMATION / TRAINING		
Les Entrepreneurs de l'Audiovisuel Européen – **EAVE**	M. Raymond RAVAR Rue Thérésienne, 8 – B-1000 BRUXELLES	TEL.: (2) 511.90.32 FAX: (2) 511.02.79
MEDIA Business School	Mr. Andrès VICENTE GOMEZ Velàzquez 12 (7° y 8°) E-28001 MADRID	TEL.: (1) 431 42 46 FAX: (1) 435 59 94
IV.FINANCING / FINANCEMENT		
Media Venture	M. Michel GYORY Fédération Européenne des Réalisateurs de l'Audiovisuel (FERA) Avenue Everard, 55 – B-1190 BRUXELLES	TEL.: (2) 345.74.78 FAX: (2) 344.57.80
	M. Jean Pierre BOUILLOT Société Européenne d'Ingéniérie Financière (SEFI) Boulevard Royal, 10 GDL-2449 LUXEMBOURG	TEL.: (352) 46 07 10 FAX: (352) 46 07 11

▶ *Figure 10   European Economic Community Coordinators for Media Pilot Projects.*

designated to promote the arts. For example, talk to the National Film Board of Canada.

Once you are set on your geographic location, remember that you have several levels of government to approach—local, regional, state, federal. *The AV Marketplace*, listed under publications later in this chapter, identifies some of these government agencies in the United States. How vast your options are with government agencies will depend on what country you are in. But in the United States, and a number of the industrialized democracies, if an agency at one level of government turns you down, you might well approach another agency at either the same or a different level of government.

Specialized Markets

Worldwide conventions and festivals are listed regularly in *Television International*, *TELCO*, and in *Broadcasting Magazine*.

A number have been listed in Chapter 5 in the discussion of distribution.

Aside from the festivals for entertainment, drama, educational, and documentary productions, it is also possible to find specialized festivals. Some examples are:

U.S. Industrial Film and Video Festival
841 North Addison Avenue
Elmhurst, IL 60126
Tel.: 708-834-7773
Fax: 708-834-5565

Festival of Sports Films
21 rue Patou
59800 Lille, France
Tel.: 33-20-3005-00
This festival also exhibits exploration and adventure productions.

Image Caribe
Suzie Landou, Director
77 Route de la Folie
97200, Fort de France
Martinique.
Producers and filmmakers from the Caribbean are just beginning to organize as a cultural unit. This organization's festival is the focal point.[14]

Federation of African Film Makers
Filippe Sawagogo, Secretary General
01BP254 Post Box
Ouagadougou
Burkina Faso
This organization of African producers holds an international festival in Africa every two years. Artists come from all over the world.[15]

Figure 11 is a list of national contacts for the European Economic Community EURO AIM, the organization dedicated to supporting the marketing of European indepedent productions.

Antennes / National Contacts

Belgique / Belgium:
WALLONIE BRUXELLES-IMAGES
(Marie-Anne HUPIN)
Rue des Minimes, 26 – B-1000 Bruxelles
Tel: (32) 2/518 14 60 – Fax: (32) 2/512 86 57

Danemark / Denmark:
PRODUCENTERNE (Ebbe PREISLER)
Vesterbrogade, 37 – DK-1620 Copenhagen
Tel: (45) 31/22 16 36 – Fax: (45) 31/22 06 47

Espagne / Spain:
1) NOSKI (Josu ERGUIN)
Calle Zaragoza – Pozuelo de Alarcon
E-28023 Madrid
Tel: (34) 1/711 46 11 – Fax: (34) 1/711 81 42

2) OMEYA (Antonio P. PEREZ)
Manuel Siurol 34 – E-41013 Sevilla
Tel: (34) 54/61 02 80 – Fax: (34) 54/62 80 61

3) EUROVIP (Raquel CASERO)
Nuria, S. Mirasierra – E-28034 Madrid
Tel: (34) 1/734 73 57 – Fax: (34) 1/734 76 74

4) VIDEOBAI (Mikel IBARRONDO)
Industrialdea 16 – E-20160 Lasarte (Guipuzcoa)
Tel: (34) 43/34 43 37 – Fax: (34) 43/36 39 51

5) DIRECCION GRAL. DE PROMOCION
CULTURAL CONSEJERIA DE CULTURA
Y DEPORTES
(José Antonio Coira NIETO)
Edif. San Cayetano. Bloque 3, 2a – E-15704 Santiago
Tel: (34) 81/56 60 00 – Fax: (34) 81/56 18 02

6) PYMEV – Associación de Productores de Cine
de la Comunidad Autonoma de Valencia
(José M. FERRANDIZ MOTO)
Moratin 11 entlo. pta 3
E-46002 Valencia
Tel: (34) 6/352 29 77 – Fax: (34) 6/352 49 62

7) VIRGINIA FILMS S.A. (Paco POCH)
Cardenal Sentmenat. 37 Baixos – E-08017 Barcelona
Tel: (34) 3/204 92 21 – Fax: (34) 3/205 45 58

Finlande / Finland:
TELEVISUAL COMMUNICATIONS (OURA Aki)
Unionink 45 A9
SF-00170 Helsinki
Tel.: (358) 0/135 13 00 – Fax: (358) 0/135 19 48

France:
EUROCREATION
(Anne-Marie AUTISSIER)
Rue Debelleyme, 3 – F-75003 Paris
Tel.: (33) 1/48 04 78 79
Fax: (33) 1/40 29 92 46

Grèce / Greece:
ORAMA (Lucia RIKAKI)
Nikosthenous St.. 28 – GR-11635 Athens
Tel: (30) 1/751 34 02 – Fax: (30) 1/724 93 70

Irlande / Ireland:
IRISH EXPORT BOARD (Derry O'BRIEN)
Merrion Hall. Strand Road – Sandymount. Dublin 2
Tel: (353) 1/669 50 11 – Fax: (353) 1/669 58 20

Italie / Italy:
SOFT VIDEO (Elio ANDALO)
Via Bettolo, 54 – I-00195 Roma
Tel: (39) 6/325 16 61 – Fax: (39) 6/35 34 29

Luxembourg / Luxemburg:
P.A.L. (Nicolas STEIL)
Rue de l'Eau, 18 – L-1449 Luxembourg
Tel: (352) 279 55 – Fax: (352) 279 56

Pays-Bas / The Netherlands:
FRANCA PELSTER FILMS (Franca PELSTER)
P.O. BOX 5104 – NL-1410 AC Naarden
Tel: (31) 2159/50 196 – Fax: (31) 2159/50 449
ou Breiten 33 – CH-3232 Ins
Tel: (41) 32/83 30 33 – Fax: (41) 32/83 33 68

Portugal:
COSTA do CASTELLO (Paulo TRANCOSO)
Costa do Castello. 66-68 – P-1100 Lisboa
Tel: (351) 1/87 64 39 – Fax: (351) 1/87 20 80

République Fédérale d'Allemagne / West Germany:
EX-PICTURIS (Wolfgang PFEIFFER)
Fidicinstrasse. 40 – D-1000 Berlin 61
Tel: (49) 30/691 60 08 – Fax: (49) 30/692 95 75

Royaume-Uni / United Kingdom:
1) ASSOCIATION OF INDEPENDENT PRODUCERS
(Lori KEATING)
Paramount House
162-170 Wardour Street – London W1V4LA
Tel: (44) 71/434 01 81 – Fax: (44) 71/437 00 86
2) IPPA SCOTLAND (Lowri GARLAND)
Victoria Crescent Road. 74
UK Glasgow G129JN
Tel: (41) 339/5660 – Fax: (41) 334/6519
3) TAC (Sion PYRS)
Gronant – Penrallt Isaf
Carnaervon LL551NS WALES
Tel: 286/67 11 23 – Fax: 286/77449

Suède / Sweden:
EUROMEDIA CONSULT AB
(Christina BLOMBERG)
Nybrogatan 46 VI
S 11440 Stockholm
Tel: (46) 8/667 34 20 – Fax: (46) 8/662 13 71

Suisse / Switzerland:
CENTRE SUISSE DU CINEMA
(Diana KNÖPFLE)
1, Place Bel-Air – CH-1003 Lausanne
Tel: (41) 21/311 03 23 – Fax: (41) 21/311 03 25

Yougoslavie / Yugoslavia:
INSTITUT ZA FILM (Predag GOLUBOVIC)
Cika Ljubina 15/11 – Y-11000 Belgrade
Tel: (38) 11/625 131

▶ *Figure 11 National contacts for the European Economic Community's EURO AIM.*

For those who need funding, one of the best resource libraries in the United States is the Foundation Center Library. It you can't get to New York, major metropolitan cities across the country have foundation libraries that are connected with the one in New York. Also, some local public libraries will carry some of the material available in the New York center.

The Foundation Center Library
79 Fifth Avenue
New York, NY 10003
Tel.: 212-620-4230

The library has a wide range of funding sources for organizations and for individuals. Its resources identify funders, including private foundations, corporate foundations, and individual philanthropists. The library covers every topic imaginable, so the resource lists will be broader than at those organizations specializing in video and film. One might seek funding for a project that included a co-production but also included other things. The library can also do computer searches for funders of special types of projects.

For specialized production funding, two leading American resources are the CPB Television Program Fund and the National Endowment for the Humanities. Many other funding sources also exist.

Corporation for Public Broadcasting Television Program Fund
901 E Streeet NW
Washington, DC 20004-2006
Tel.: 202-879-9600

National Endowment for the Humanities
Projects in the Media
1100 Pennsylvania Ave. NW
Washington, DC.20506
Tel.: 202-786-0278

Those interested in information about carnéts might contact:

Carnét Representative
U.S. Council for International Business
1212 Avenue of the Americas, 21st Floor
New York, N.Y 10036-1689
Tel.: 212-354-4480
Fax: 212-575-0327.

A.T.A Carnéts is a term used in both French and English is for identifying temporary documents in order to eliminate posting taxes on duties when entering a foreign country when merchandise might otherwise be called commercial samples or professional equipment.

For information about production insurance contact:

Cohen Insurance
225 West 34th Street
New York, NY 10001

Ask for a copy of the booklet called "What You Should Know about Production Insurance."

Publications

Film and Video Finder
National Information Center for Educational Media
Access Innovations, Inc.
c/o Plexus Publishing, Inc.
143 Old Marlton Pike, Medford, NJ 08055
The second edition, published in 1989, lists names and addresses of hundreds of producers and distributors.

AV Market Place, 1991
prepared by R.R. Bowker's Database
The Publications Systems Department
630 Central Ave.
New Providence, NJ 07974
This book is a complete business directory of American audio, audiovisual, computer systems, film and video resources, complete with industry yellow pages. It also lists government agencies that provide services for film and video producers.

The TELCO Report
2730 Wilshire Blvd.
Suite 404
Santa Monica, CA 90403
Tel.: 213-828-4003
Fax: 213-828-3340
See the description in Chapter 5.

Television International
P.O. Box 2430
Hollywood, CA 90028
Tel: 818-795-8386
Fax: 818-795-8436
This is one of the few periodicals devoted totally to international television.

World Radio TV Handbook
Billboard Publications
1515 Broadway
New York, NY 10036
This book provides information on broadcasters and on world TV standards.

Broadcasting Magazine
1735 DeSales Street, NW
Washington, DC 20036
This weekly industry magazine provides much information on current activities in the profession.

Independent Film and Video Monthly
625 Broadway, 9th Floor
New York, NY 10012
This is the AIVF magazine.

Program Producer's Handbook
PBS Programming
1320 Braddock Place
Alexandria, VA 22314
Tel.: 703-739-5060

Motion Picture TV and Theatre Directory
Motion Picture Enterprises Publications, Inc.
Tarrytown, NY 10591
Tel.: 212-245-0969

The Creative Black Book, 1991: Producer's Volume
Division of SRDS, Inc.
115 5th Avenue
New York, NY 10003
Tel.: 212-254-1330
Fax: 212-598-4497
This is a directory of creative talent for producers in video, film and for post-production work.

Catalogue of Federal Domestic Assistance
U.S. Government Printing Office
Washington, DC 20402
These may no longer be available on an annual basis, but use an older copy, together with a current copy of the *U.S. Budget* (also available from this office in Washington or from government bookstores located in certain major U.S. cities). You will be able to identify the full list of U.S. government funded programs.

Foundation Directory
The Foundation Center Library
79 Fifth Avenue
New York, NY 10003
Tel.: 212-620-4230
This book is updated regularly and provides a description of American based foundations—many of which also fund international programs. A comparable directory of corporations that make charitable contributions is also available.

In addition, there are production directories that tell you what resources are available in a given city. Contact people working in production in a given area to identify the best local listing. ITVA and other organizations have resource guides for their members.

International Stations
The list in Figure 12 includes contact stations in a number of countries where other references have not been provided in this book. They are listed as a starting

point for the co-producer who needs to identify with whom to work in a given area, or through whom a product might be distributed.

In conclusion, you can supplement the resources listed here. Ask those with whom you speak for names they have on their individual Rolladexes. Use your imagination to determine new ways to obtain the information you need for the project and location that concerns you.

ALGERIA
  Enterprise Nationale de Television
  (ENTV)
  21 Boulevard des Martyrs
  BP 184 El-Mouradia
  Alger, Algeria
  Fax: 213-2-590270
AUSTRALIA
  Australian Broadcasting Corporation
  ABC House
  GPO Box 9994
  Sydney, Australia
  Fax: 61-2-3565305
BARBADOS
  Caribbean Broadcasting Corporation
  The Pine
  St. Michael
  P.O. Box 900
  Bridgetown, Barbados
  Fax: 809-4292171
BRAZIL
  TV Globo LTDA
  Rua Lopes Quintas 303
  22.463 Rio de Janeiro–RJ, Brazil
  Fax: 55-21-2949182
BULGARIA
  Balgarska Televizija
  Blv. Dr Cankov 4
  BG-Sofia, Bulgaria
  Fax: 359-2-871871
CHILE
  Corporacion de Television de la
  Universidad Catolica de Chile
  Ines Matte Urrejola 0848
  Casilla 14600
  Santiago, Chile
  Fax: 56-2-377044
CYPRUS
  Cyprus Broadcasting Corporation
  Broadcasting House
  P.O. Box 4824
  Nicosia, Cyprus
  Fax: 357-2-314050

CZECHOSLOVAKIA
  Ceskoslovenske Televize (CST)
  Gorkeho nam. 29-30
  CS-11150 Praha 1, Czechoslovakia
  Fax: 42-2-2364435
DENMARK
  Danmark Radio, TV Centre
  Moerkhoejvej 170
  DK-2860
  Soeborg, Denmark
  Fax: 45-3-9661036
EGYPT
  Egypt Radio and Television Union
  Radio and Television Building
  Corniche El Nil
  Maspero
  Cairo 1186, Egypt
  Fax: 20-2-746989
FINLAND
  TV-1 YLE
  Radio and Television Centre
  Radiokatu 5
  POB 10
  SF-00241 Helsinki 24, Finland
  Fax: 358-0-1525148
HONG KONG
  Asia Television LTD.
  Television House
  81 Broadcast Drive
  Kowloon, Hong Kong
  Fax: 852-338-0438
HUNGARY
  Magyar Televizio (MTV)
  Szabadsag ter 17
  H-1810 Budapest 5, Hungary
  Fax: 36-1-1574979
ISRAEL
  Israel Broadcasting Authority
  Television Jerusalem
  P.O. Box 7139
  IL-Jersualem, Israel
  Fax: 972-2-242944

(*continued*)

▶ *Figure 12*   *Some television stations outside the United States.*

JAMAICA
  Jamaica Broadcasting Corporation
  Radio and Television Centre
  5 South Odeaon Avenue
  P.O. Box 100
  Kingston 10, Jamaica
  Fax: 809-9291029
JAPAN
  Asahi National Broadcasting Company
  LTD.
  1-1-1 Roppongi
  Minato-ku
  Tokyo 106, Japan
  Fax: 81-3-35053539
JORDAN
  Jordan Radio and Television
  Corporation
  P.O. Box 2333
  Amman, Jordan
  Fax: 962-6-788115
SOUTH KOREA
  Korean Broadcasting System
  31 Yoido-dong, Youngdungpo-gu
  Seoul 150-728, Korea
  Fax: 82-2-7857225
KUWAIT
  Kuwait Broadcasting and Television
  Service
  Ministry of Information
  P.O. Box 193 Safat
  13002 Safat, Kuwait
  Fax: 965-2421926
MEXICO
  Instituto Mexicano de Television
  Av. Periferico Sur No. 4121
  Fuentes de Pedregal
  14141 Mexico DF, Mexico
MOROCCO
  Radiodiffusion Television Morocco
  1 rue El Brihi
  Rabat, Morocco
  Fax: 212-7-762-010
NEW ZEALAND
  Television New Zealand LTD.
  Television Centre
  100 Victorial Street West
  P.O. Box 3819
  Auckland, New Zealand
  Fax: 64-9-750918

POLAND
  Polski Radio I Televwizja
  Ul. J.P. Woronicza 17
  PL-00-950 Warzawa P-35, Poland
  Fax: 48-22-440206
ROMANIA
  Contact via Press Attache
  Romanian embassy most convenient
  (If in U.S., contact Washington, DC;
  if in Europe, contact den Haag, The
  Netherlands)
SPAIN
  Radiotelevision Espanola
  Casa de la Radio
  E-28023 Madrid, Spain
  Fax: 34-1-7114509
SYRIA
  Organisme de la Radio-Television
  Syrienne
  TV and Broadcasting Directorate
  Ommayad Square
  Damascus, Syria
TURKEY
  Turkiye Radyo Televizyon Kurumu
  Nevzat Tandogan Caddesi 2
  Kavaklidere-Ankara, Turkey
  Fax: 90-4-191109
YUGOSLAVIA
  Jugoslovenska Radiotelevizija
  General Zdanova 28
  BP 284
  YU-11000 Beograd, Yugoslavia
  Fax: 38-11-434021
SAUDI ARABIA
  Saudi Arabian Television
  P.O. Box 57137
  Riyadh 11574, Saudi Arabia
  Fax: 966-1-4054176
VENEZUELA
  Radio Caracas Television
  Apartado 2057
  Dolores a Puente Soublette
  Caracas 1010 A, Venezuela
  Fax: 58-2-412294
ZIMBABWE
  Zimbabwe Broadcasting Corporation
  P.O. Box HG 444
  Highlands
  Harare, Zimbabwe

► *Figure 12*   (*continued*)

Notes

1. Personal interview with Dighton E. Spooner, Jr., Executive Vice President, Films for Television, Grenada Television, 36 Golden Square, London W1R 4AH, England, fax: 213-282-8992, tel.: 213-282-8996, February 15, 1991.

2. Personal interview with Jim Stevenson, Chief Executive, Educational Broadcasting Services Trust, 1/2 Marylebone High Street, London W1A 1AR, England, fax: 01-224-2426, tel.: 01-927-5023, February 15, 1991.

3. Personal interview with Dr. Leonid A. Zolotarevsky, Director, Department for International Programming, U.S.S.R. National State Broadcasting Company, Moscow, Russia, June 13, 1991.

4. Spooner interview.

5. Personal interview with Lydia Stephans, Director, Programming, ABC Sports, 47 West 66th Street, New York, NY 10023, tel.: 212-456-3702, August 23, 1991.

6. Personal interview with Tony Goodman, Deputy Director, IVCA, Bolsover House, 5/6 Clipstone St., London W1P 7EB, England, February 15, 1991.

7. Personal interview with Alain Jehlan, Director of Acquisitions, "Nova," WGBH, Boston, August 27, 1991.

8. Spooner interview.

9. Personal interview with Susan Ryan, Independent Distribution Consultant, 3285 33rd St., #B1, Astoria, NY 11106, August 22, 1991.

10. Personal interview with Herb Fuller, independent filmmaker, 54 Preston Road, Somerville, MA 02143, August 13, 1991.

11. Telephone interview with Peter Vesey, Vice President, CNN International, One CNN Center, Atlanta, GA 30303, November 12, 1991.

12. The IVCA Magazine (IVCA, Bolsover House, 5/6 Clipstone Street, London W1P 7EB, England, tel.: 44-71-580-0962, fax: 44-71-436-2606), February 1991.

13. "International Flavor," Broadcasting, Vol. 119, No. 17, October 22, 1990, p. 88.

14. Personal interview with Professor Claire Andrade Watkins, Wellesley College and Emerson College, Boston, Mass., October 16, 1991.

15. Watkins interview.

7

▼ Conclusions

If you are starting a career in television co-production, you need to answer three questions:

1. What are your goals? What kind of a world do you want to make for yourself, your generation, and your children's generation? Can you improve global understanding and peace among people of differing backgrounds? Can you do anything to ensure that shortages of food and housing are eliminated, or to help to free the world from epidemics? Do you have a talent to produce entertainment or sports to lift the quality of life for people across the globe? How can you upgrade the levels of economic prosperity for the communities around you and thereby for yourself?

2. What are your objectives? That is, what specific activities will enable you to fulfill your particular goals? Assuming that you view television as the medium for carrying your message, how will you use TV? What's the most effective, most creative way to use television to its fullest potential— to combine the human resources and the technology to produce programs? Is it with entertainment, or news, or documentaries? Is it in producing programs for broadcast, for corporate and educational teleconferences, for video cassette publishing, or something newer still?

3. What methods can be useful to you as you turn your ideas and ideals into real products for the marketplace? Is co-production a tool that can enhance the quality of your work?

While it may be the exception rather than the rule for a young professional in America to think about her or his career in so deliberate a fashion, those who take the time to develop such a plan for themselves are often the ones who have the most sucessful careers both personally and in terms of what they contribute to the larger society.

The thesis of this book is that international television co-production is a tool that deserves increased use as we enter the global neighborhood of the 21st century. Co-production is useful for several reasons:

1. Television station ownership is becoming international. As that happens it becomes increasingly important for persons with very differing cultural backgrounds to learn to work as collaborating partners. Otherwise, we'll magnify civilization's problems by widening the gap between the owners and the owned.

2. Producing quality entertainment programming has become extremely expensive. Television audiences see Hollywood as the standard. Lesser quality cannot be successfully competitive. As the global economies struggle with the problems of the 1980s and 1990s, either producers will find ways to do quality programming for less cost or quality will suffer. Co-production cuts cost.

3. There's a proliferation of television channels throughout the world as a result of satellite technology, fiber optics, and political changes making new markets accessible. These outlets need new programming. Co-production is one way of providing the programming that blends the cultural integrity and skill development of people in one area with the seasoned television technology experience and the resources from another area.

4. New technologies and new industries are on the horizon. Interactive video, videodiscs, video publishing, and the flexibility in programming that is possible with fiber optics. How these technologies can be used to their fullest potential in the marketplace remains to be seen. But in a global neighborhood, international collaboration makes possible added creativity in program design and distribution, added markets to which to distribute, added opportunity for educational and documentary production, added flexibility for corporate, government, and institutional communication, added possibilities for entertainment programming, and more colleagues with whom to build solid, successful professional enterprises.

Co-production can offer exciting career possibilities, as can the whole arena of international television in the next decade. The key to success, however, lies in knowing not to consider co-production an end in itself but as a tool to achieve other goals. As Dighton Spooner, Grenada Television's Vice President, Films for Television, warned, "Work from the creative to co-production, rather than the other way around."[1]

Start with an idea, a dream, a goal. Find your own way to harness these ideas with the most appropriate technology so that a quality product conveys the message, whether your objective is to do that through a program, a series of programs, or a business venture. Your imagination, your ability to develop creative programs, and your career in the competitive marketplace will benefit from such a global perspective.

Jump into the international waters of co-production. Remember the words of independent filmmaker Herb Fuller, "If you get someone to pay for it, do it often. If you have to pay for it yourself, do it at least once."[2]

Notes

1. Personal interview with Dighton E. Spooner, Jr., Executive Vice President, Films for Television, Grenada Television, 36 Golden Square, London W1R 4AH, England, fax: 213-282-8992, tel.: 213-282-8996, February 15, 1991.
2. Personal interview with Herb Fuller, independent filmmaker, 54 Preston Road, Somerville, MA 02143, August 13, 1991.

Index